St. Bonaventure's

On the Reduction of the Arts to Theology

Translation with Introduction and Commentary

WORKS OF SAINT BONAVENTURE

Series Edited by
F. Edward Coughlin, O.F.M.

St. Bonaventure's

On the Reduction of the Arts to Theology

Translation with Introduction and Commentary

Prepared by

Zachary Hayes, O.F.M.

Franciscan Institute
St. Bonaventure University
St. Bonaventure, N.Y. 14778

1996

Library of Congress Catalog Card Number

96–086751

ISBN: 1–57659–043–7

Printed in the United States of America
    BookMasters
    Ashland, Ohio

Table of Contents

FOREWORD

The original copyright on the first volume of this series goes back to 1940. A second edition is dated in 1955. The first version of this volume was the work of Sr. Emma Thérèse Healy, a member of the Congregation of the Sisters of St. Joseph, Erie, Pennsylvania. That edition has been virtually normative as an English-language translation with introduction and commentary since its original publication.

In the intervening years, there have been many studies on the thought and spirituality of St. Bonaventure. It was felt that a reworking of the pertinent material would be in place at this time. Also, the format of the original edition has proven somewhat awkward for those attempting to use it. This is due, at least in part, to the fact that the text of the *De reductione* is unusually brief: a mere seven pages in the Quaracchi edition. This means that the argument of the text is extremely tight and would be virtually unintelligible for a person who was not already well-read in medieval thought patterns. To make the text more accessible, the Healy edition placed the text itself in the context of a detailed essay which functions partly as an introduction and partly as an essay-style commentary. In this way it was possible to publish this as an independent volume containing much valuable information about the intellectual world of Bonaventure. Unfortunately, the text itself tended to get lost in this format.

With this in mind, we have attempted to provide a format that might be easier to follow, though it would not have much of the detail offered by the Healy edition. Using that earlier edition as the basis, we have made numerous changes in the translation itself. We have reduced the material in the introduction and have made major changes in the issues discussed as introductory. Finally, we have offered an essay-style commentary which is divided into sections that correspond precisely to the structure of the text. At times in this commentary we have incorporated sections of the Healy edition when this seemed appropriate. But much of the material has been reformulated in the light of more recent studies.

It is our hope that this format will provide an inexpensive edition of this remarkable medieval text with sufficient background information to make it readily available and usable for those involved in studies on the history of Western Christian thought.

Zachary Hayes, OFM
Chicago, IL
October, 1996

INTRODUCTION

I. *Title, occasion, sources.*

a) *Title.*

The title of this small work of Bonaventure is itself the expression of the life-time project of the Master. It implies the long-standing conviction of the Seraphic Doctor that the ideal for the spiritual-intellectual life is to draw all the varied forms of human knowledge into a unity to serve the human person in the spiritual journey. This project rests on the assumption that all the forms of knowledge as then known are to be related finally to divine revelation which is the highest form of wisdom and is the concern of Scripture or theology.

The idea of *reduction* in Bonaventure's world of thought has both a metaphysical and a cognitive significance. As a metaphysical term, the word has to do with the circle of creation as it emanates from God eventually to return to its point of origin. The idea of the return is expressed in the word *reduction* which means literally *leading back*. In its final consummation, creation is led back to its point of origin in God. As a cognitive term, the word refers to the way in which the human subject comes to know and understand the realities of the created order in the light of this metaphysical conviction. But as a human venture, this should not be allowed to become simply a neutral knowledge. Rather, the journey of human cognition is best understood as one dimension of the way in which the human, spiritual journey is involved in creation's return to God. Therefore it has no independent significance.

The term *arts*, as is clear from Bonaventure's text, is here taken in a broader sense and is not limited simply to the liberal arts. In the present case, Bonaventure includes not only the academic disciplines but the so-called mechanical arts as well. As all knowledge is led back to the the deepest wisdom of the Scriptures which is elaborated in the form of theology, the human subject tracing this route is led to the fuller awareness of the mystery of the love from which all has taken its origin. Thus, the journey leads not only to knowledge but finally to loving union with the mystery of creative love from which all things emanate.

Theology, as understood here, is difficult to distinguish from Scripture. This can be seen even in the language used by medieval authors. Often, *sacra doctrina* and *theologia* are used interchangeably with *revelatio* or *sacra Scriptura*. All of these words are used not so much to distinguish particular theological disciplines as to distinguish Christian faith from the teachings of philosophy and other secular sciences. In the prologue to the *Breviloquium*, for example, Bonaventure describes the content of theology as "the origin, development, and end of sacred Scripture."[1] We might say that at this point in Western history prior to the emergence of the many distinct, specialized theological disciplines familiar to us, theology was understood to be intimately tied to the Scriptures. At the time of Bonaventure's studies at Paris, one would have first studied the arts. After this, if one wished to study theology, one would have studied the Scriptures. And finally, one would have studied the *Sentences* of Peter Lombard.

At this point, it might be helpful to recall the nature of the *Sentences*. Simply put, the *Sentences* amounted to a collection of the views of the Fathers, largely those of Augustine, gathered from commentaries on the Scriptures and other writings. From this we can conclude that, even at this level, theology is virtually inseparable from the Scriptures, even though the text which is the direct concern of the commentator on the *Sentences* is several steps removed from the actual text of the Scriptures. While one might say that for this period of intellectual history, theology is best understood to be the proper understanding of the Scriptures, there may be considerable difference of opinion as to what is the most appropriate key to unlock that meaning.

To lead the arts back to theology means, for Bonaventure, to show the organic connection between all the arts and the central concern of the Scriptures or theology. None of the arts, including philosophy, ought to be allowed to stand as an independent and self-sufficient discipline. All ought to be brought into relation to the highest form of wisdom available to human beings in this life:

---

[1] *Brevil.*, prol. (V, 201).

namely, theology. Only then will all forms of human knowledge serve effectively in realizing the true end of human existence.

b) *Occasion.*

It is impossible to give a precise date for the composition of this work. Some scholars are inclined to see it as an early work in which Bonaventure sketched out his future program. Others are inclined to see it as quite late since it seems to bring into such elegant unity the entire dynamic of the Seraphic Doctor's life-project. J. Bougerol suggests that this may well have been the final work of Bonaventure in which he summarized what he had been attempting to do in much greater detail in the *Collations on the Hexaemeron*.[2] However we try to resolve the question of dating, the fact is that this text hardly seems to be an immature work. This becomes very clear if it is compared with works such as the *Itinerarium*, the *Collations on the Gifts of the Spirit*, and the *Collations on the Hexaemeron* all of which carry out a similar project in greater or lesser detail.

A possible hint concerning the time of composition may be found in the fourth of Bonaventure's *Collations on the Gifts of the Holy Spirit*. There in discussing the gift of knowledge, Bonaventure speaks of the philosophical disciplines and states that there is nothing in these disciplines which does not imply a vestige of the Trinity. He follows this with the cryptic remark: "This would be easy to show, but it would take a long time." The editors of the Quaracchi edition have suggested that this text might be seen as a *promise* which found fulfillment in the form of the *De reductione*. If this is the case, it would place its composition relatively late in the Master's life. The *Collations on the Gifts of the Holy Spirit* are commonly dated to the year 1269 which is just a few years prior to the *Collations on the Hexaemeron* which carry out the proposal in the most elaborate form imaginable in 1273.

---

[2] Cfr. J. Bougerol, *Introduction to Bonaventure* (St. Anthony Guild Press, 1961) p. 163. (Now available from Franciscan Press at Quincy University, Quincy, IL).

c) *Sources.*

The most obvious patristic source one might suspect in dealing with the work of Bonaventure would be the writings of St. Augustine. But if we distinguish the general Augustinian background from citations of specific works, we might conclude that the influence of Augustine is not as massive in the present text as we might have supposed. A far more obvious influence in the structure of this text and the delineation of the arts contained in it would be the work of the twelfth-century monk, Hugh of St. Victor, who is chronologically much closer to Bonaventure. The works of Hugh which stand out in this context are the *Expositio in Hierarchiam Coelestem S. Dionysii Areopagitae* and the *Eruditio Didascalica.*[3] Taking this into account, we might conclude that key elements in the composition of the *De reductione* have historical roots in the writings of the sixth-century Christian neo-Platonist, Pseudo-Dionysius, and are mediated through Dionysius's twelfth-century interpreter, Hugh of St. Victor. Hugh lays out the various stages of knowledge involved in the soul's journey toward the fullest and most perfect form of contemplation in a way that seems to be clearly echoed in the text of Bonaventure.

II. *Some elements in Bonaventure's world-view.*

In order to understand the logical structure and development of the *De reductione,* it is important to read it with at least some general sense of the world-view of Bonaventure. Our intention is not to provide a very detailed discussion of the physics and the metaphysics of the Seraphic Doctor, but simply to highlight particular themes that clearly pertain to the text under consideration.

a) *Light metaphysics.*

If, on the one hand, there is a tendency to think of God in the symbolism of light, and on the other hand to think of creation in terms of the neo-Platonic concept of emanation, it is not difficult to think of God's creative work as the emanation of light from its

---

[3] Cfr. Migne (PL 175, 923-1154); and (PL 176, 741-838).

supreme, fontal source (=the Godhead) outward toward the darkness of nothingness thus calling finite reality into existence. This raises the issue of the metaphysics of light, a problem which may seem particularly obscure to the modern reader but which is basic in the understanding of the argument of the *De reductione*.

It was common for Christian scholars of the thirteenth century to assume some form of hylomorphic theory as a way of accounting for the existence of changeable beings as they are experienced in the world. But there were various forms of hylomorphism available at the time of Bonaventure's academic career. For Bonaventure, all creatures are composed of matter and form, matter being the determinable principle and form being the determining principle. But more specifically, Bonaventure held to the theory of a plurality of forms. And in this context, he held that light was the first and most noble form of all finite beings, some partaking in it more deeply than others, but all being involved to some degree. Light, he writes, can be viewed from three perspectives. Considered in itself as the first form of all bodies, it is called *lux*. In as far as it radiates from the being which it informs, it is called *lumen*. And when it is viewed in terms of the terminal point at which it becomes perceptible it is called *color*.[4]

Light, it will be recalled, was created on the first day according to the *Genesis* account (*Gn.* 1: 3), even before the sun and the other heavenly bodies. While light is not itself a body in the strict sense, it is for Bonventure the first form of all bodies, and its influence extends throughout the entire material universe. It is involved even in the formation of the earthly minerals, and it is through the influence of light that all complex bodies are generated out of the basic minerals. Different kinds of bodies, therefore, are arranged in a hierarchy in accordance with the degree of their participation in light. Light, then, is the principle of perfection in all corporal beings, and is responsible for their beauty, color, and activity.

This understanding of light, commonly referred to as light-metaphysics, is not original to Bonaventure. For much of this he is indebted especially to Robert Grosseteste and to the Oxford Franciscans, and more proximately to his mentor at Paris,

---

[4] *I Sent.* d. 17, p. 1, q.1 (I, 294).

Alexander of Hales. Elements of this theory can be traced back to particular readings of Augustine, to the neo-Platonism of Plotinus, and perhaps even to Plato's comparison of the Idea of the Good with the sun.

If we think of light in terms of the way in which it can be focused in a very sharp and intense point, and how it radiates from that point outward in all directions, we may be well on the way to an understanding of the manner in which Bonaventure uses the language of light to speak of truth and knowledge in the text which we are considering here. The Primal Light is God. And that Light is identical with Truth. From that divine source, light and truth radiate outward in the direction of creation and to the finite mind. There is in the world of creation a corporal light and a created, spiritual light which can be compared in a limited way with God, the divine Light.

b) *The metaphysics of Bonaventure: Emanation, exemplarity, reduction.*

In his final work, Bonaventure makes the explicit statement: "This is the whole of our metaphysics: it is about emanation, exemplarity, and consummation; that is, to be illumined by spiritual rays and to be led back to the supreme Being."[5] And he follows this with: "Any person who is unable to consider how things originate, how they are led back to their end, and how God shines forth in them, is incapable of achieving true understanding."[6]

Here is the neo-Platonic circle of origin and end which played such an emphatic role in the creation-theology of medieval Christian theologians. And for Bonaventure, between the point of origin and the point of end stands the mystery of exemplarity. When the Christian doctrine of creation is developed within this framework, the implication is that as finite being emerges from its fontal source in the creative love of God, it is drawn along the circle of return to its final goal, its consummation being found in a loving union with the divine. If we do not understand this, regardless of

---

[5] *Hex.* 2, 17 (V, 332).
[6] *Hex.* 3, 2 (V, 343).

how much specific information we may have about particular beings, we do not really understand them in terms of their deepest meaning.

Distinctive of Bonaventure's metaphysics is the way in which it emphasizes the importance of exemplarity. This is the central issue in his metaphysical circle. For him, the question of exemplarity is first of all a philosophical question. But the ultimate answer to this philosophical question does not become available to humans until the eternal archetype becomes enfleshed in the history of Jesus. It follows, therefore, that the final answer to the question of exemplarity is found at the level of faith and theology. It is a christological answer. The implication of this will become clear in the text under consideration as we note how frequently the mystery of the incarnation surfaces in the presentation of Bonaventure.

At the metaphysical level, we might say that as creation emerges out of the depths of the divine, creative love it gives external expression to that primal, internal self-expression of God found in the eternal Word. This takes us into the realm of trinitarian theology. Here it is Bonaventure's view that at the level of God's primal Word of self-expression, there is but one Word. And in that one Word is contained all that the divine mystery is within itself as a mystery of self-communicative love, and all that can come to be should the divine determine to communicate itself externally. Thus, internally and in terms of logical denotation, there is but one divine Word. But in terms of logical connotation, that single Word expresses the plurality of creatures in the cosmos external to God. It is for this reason that we commonly speak of a plurality of divine Ideas, even though, in the most fundamental sense, there is but one Idea. And these Ideas are, for Bonaventure, the perfect originals after which all the limited copies in the world are created. This means that all the objects of knowledge which we encounter in the world are most truly known when they are known precisely as external expressions or symbols of the eternal Ideas.

So it is that creation is said to reflect something of the Word of God's self-expression that has become incarnate in Jesus Christ, and that creation returns to the depths of the divine love in and through its increasing conformity to the incarnate Word. This is the heart of the *reduction* by which all reality is led back to its fontal source. It is, in essence, a real movement of created reality from its source to its goal as well as a movement of knowledge which raises this movement to a conscious, cognitive level.

Since this can be known in its fullness only from the perspective of faith, it follows that all knowledge about the created realm, no matter how mundane the object of knowledge might seem to be, will find its ultimate significance only when it is seen in terms of this great movement of the whole created order. Thus, it becomes clear why Bonaventure can respect the insights of all the human cognitive disciplines on the one hand, and yet see them as limited and in need of the insights of faith and theology on the other hand. This position plays a major role not only in the title but also in the entire structure of the *De reductione,* as will become clear later.

c) *Learning and sanctity.*

Of fundamental importance for understanding the argument of the *De reductione* is the role of learning and the relation between learning and sanctity in the thought of Bonaventure. Bonaventure lived at a time when the centuries-long monastic tradition with its sense of a unified vision of study in the context of monastic life was being challenged by the emergence of the newly founded universities situated in the growing urban centers of medieval Europe. This change of locale coincided with the problems raised by Aristotle's philosophical thought and the inroads of Islamic and Jewish scholarship into the world of the universities. The thirteenth century would see a variety of approaches to these problems. Bonaventure would become known as the champion of the unity of Christian wisdom, even though the attempt to maintain such a position would be much more complex than it had been in the world of monastic spirituality and theology.

A number of times during his career, Bonaventure treated the issue of scholarly work in a very direct manner. Perhaps the most telling discussion appears in his *Collations on the Gifts of the Holy Spirit,* specifically in the fourth *Collation* on the gift of knowledge. As we read that text, we can hear the ideal of the familiar monastic tradition in the background together with the foreground voices of the new library of the learning which was becoming a living presence in the world of the university. Clearly Bonaventure was an intellectual. But just as clearly, he saw the point of intellectual training to be integrated within a wider vision of the human person and the goal of human life. Outside the world of the biblical revelation the nature of that goal remains always an open question. But within the world of revelation, faith opens the vision of a final destiny with God that transcends even what the great Plato and Aristotle were able to think of as the final destiny of humanity.

Learning, therefore, is an important element in the spiritual journey, at least for certain people; though not necessarily for all. But even for those whose way to God includes the discipline of the intellectual life, the goal of intellectual culture is not knowledge for the sake of knowledge. Nor is it knowledge for the sake of the market place. Nor is it knowledge for the sake of fame and popularity. Reaching back to the writings of St. Bernard and extending the text of that twelfth-century monastic master, Bonaventure writes:

> There are those who wish to know so that they might build up others; and this is charity. And there are those who wish to know so that they themselves may be built up; and that is prudence. Knowledge puffs up; but charity builds up. It is necessary, therefore, to join charity with knowledge so that a person might have both knowledge and charity at the same time.[7]

For Bonaventure, the important issue is, above all, knowledge integrated into the spiritual journey toward love; love of God and love of one's fellow human beings. It is clear that Bonaventure had a high regard for the intellectual life, but he never envisioned knowledge independently of the only goal that the human person finally has: loving union with God. For whatever secondary reasons a person may be engaged in studies, this primary reason should never be lost sight of. The deepest meaning of all intellectual effort is to be found in the deepening of our sense of the mystery that is God, and increasing our love for God. For

---

[7] *De donis Sp. S.* 4, 23-24 (V, 478).

Bonvaventure, knowledge is never its own end. It must eventually open into the experience of love for the divine reality in whose love all of creation is grounded. "Love reaches further than vision."[8] "Of what use is it to know many things and to savor nothing?"[9] This program of Bonaventure is pre-eminently a wisdom-tradition which sees the intellectual life to be situated within a larger context of values that ought to shape human life.

---

[8] *II Sent*. d. 23, a.2, q.3, ad 4 (II, 545).

[9] *Hex*. 22, 21 (V, 440).

Commentary on the Text

I. *General argument of the text.*

In a mere seven pages of the Quaracchi edition, Bonaventure argues concerning the relation of all forms of secular knowledge to the study of Scripture, or to theology. In doing so, he incorporates all the familiar and new forms of knowledge in the arts and sciences into an all-embracing, theological framework and integrates them into the journey of the human spirit into God. All must be situated in the context of the going-forth from and the return of creation to God. Bonaventure thus presents a thought-provoking charter for any serious form of Christian spirituality and education. He argues, in effect, that spirituality and theology do not have to by-pass or bracket the so-called secular disciplines in order to find God elsewhere; for the entire world is drenched with the presence of the divine mystery. It is a world that bears at least the vestiges (=foot–prints) of God, and at some levels even the image and the similitude of God. It is the task of the human person situated in such a world to learn how to detect the symptoms of that mysterious, divine presence. Why do human beings find it so difficult to do this? For Bonaventure, the answer to this lies in the mystery of our fallen nature which has distorted our vision and deformed our intellectual capacities. Once these have been reformed through the grace and light of Christ, we will again be able to read the glorious book of creation in which we come to know God precisely as creator, and to see the relation of creation to salvation, which is the primary concern of the book of the biblical revelation. This theme we will see running throughout the whole of the *De reductione*.

In essence, the argument of the *De reductione* looks like a broader version of the argument Bonaventure carried out especially in his later years against the radical philosophical movement. By that time, it had become specifically an argument against any claims to the self-sufficiency of philosophy. A philosophy which ignores the world of faith and theology will most likely be incomplete. It may also be seriously distorted. Therefore, the world of philosophy must always be open to further insight and to possible correction in the light of revelation.

While the strong focus on the issue of philosophy is obvious in the *Collations on the Gifts of the Holy Spirit* and finds its strongest expression in the *Collations on the Hexaemeron*, the same concern can be detected in the *De reductione*, but here in reference to the entire range of human disciplines. All of them may be seen to be important sources of insight and truth, but none of them individually nor all of them together can be seen as adequate. All must be seen, finally, in relation to the basic insights of the biblical revelation.

This is not to be taken as a form of anti-intellectualism. Bonaventure sees the human intellect as an outstanding gift of God, and all knowledge gained through the use of that faculty is truly a gift from God. Yet, as we have seen, he frowns on knowledge for its own sake. And he urges his scholarly colleagues to avoid "idle curiosity." Important as the intellectual life appears to be for Bonaventure, it is clear that no form of secular knowledge, including that of philosophy, will be sufficient in itself. All knowledge should eventually lead to and find its fulfillment in the knowledge of the Scriptures and theology. But even that is not sufficient, for knowledge itself is not the end of the soul's journey. It is Bonaventure's conviction that knowledge should move to love and to union with God. Only when that is the case does the soul truly "come home."

We can see this text, therefore, as a pre-eminent statement of the vision of a unified Christian wisdom which echoes the ancient monastic tradition but places it in a significantly new context. There are, so argues Bonaventure, three foundational elements in the biblical revelation. These are: (1) the eternal generation of the Word in the life of the triune God, and the incarnation of that same Word in Jesus of Nazareth; (2) the fundamental pattern for human life; (3) and the goal of human life as a transforming love-union with God. The general flow of the argument throughout the *De reductione* will be to highlight the analogical relations between the insights of the arts and these three concerns of the biblical tradition. In essence, this is the logic of the *reduction*.

II. *Setting the stage for the reduction* (#1-7).

#1. The text of the *Epistle of James*.

Bonaventure appeals to a biblical text which plays a significant role elsewhere in his writings.[1] It is an ideal text to set up the framework of light and illumination which undergirds the whole of the *De reductione*. God is seen here as the source of every good and perfect gift, and as the fontal source of all light and illumination.

Concerning this biblical text, Hugh of St. Victor discusses the same text at some length. This text together with expressions such as *Omnis illuminatio ab uno lumine; et multi sunt radii, et unum lumen*[2] indicate the source from which Bonaventure may have borrowed his fourfold light. It is interesting to note Hugh's distinction between natural and supernatural knowledge,[3] and his frequent use of the term *reductio*.[4]

The citation of the text of *James* with its emphasis on the gifts of God is especially appropriate to set the stage for Bonaventure's theology of creation. For Bonaventure, the whole universe is the object of God's never-failing prodigality. But it is particularly on humanity that God sends an unceasing shower of benefits. God does this without diminishing the infinite resources of the divine nature in itself. Infinitely happy independently of the created world, God cannot seek from without a happiness which is already given within in an infinite measure. Neither does God act out of self-interest.[5] Liberality, therefore, inspires all of God's acts. It is for this reason that everything that comes from God deserves the name of gift. In this sense, the whole of creation, and all the goods that humanity in particular possesses, whatever they may be, are gifts of God.[6]

---

[1] Cfr. the *Itinerarium* (V, 295) and the *Vitis Mystica* (VIII, 189) as well as *De donis S. S.*, 1, 4 (V, 458).

[2] *Expositio in Hierarchiam Coelestem S. Dionysii Areopagitae*, lib. II, Migne, PL 175, col. 935.

[3] *Ibid.*, col. 941.

[4] *Ibid.*, col. 937.

[5] I *Sent.*, d. 18, q.3, f.4, (I, 327a).

[6] *IV Sent.* D. 33, dub. VI (IV, 764a).

The same biblical text employs the metaphor of light. Thinking of the way in which physical light radiates from a point of concentration, and reaches in all directions, Bonaventure, following Hugh, can refer to God as the *fount of light* from whom the many beams of light flow out to creation. At this point, the background of light-metaphysics will help in understanding his thought. As light flows out from God, it eventually flows into the human intellect which is thus enabled to come to a deeper understanding of reality. Thus, with the natural light of the human mind and the supernatural light of grace, the human person can move along the path of human wisdom to the true Wisdom, which is Christ. This has to do with the return of the soul to God in as far as this takes place, at least in part, through knowledge.

In an introductory way, Bonaventure now presents the four lights around which he will lay out the arts and their relation to theology. His thought moves from the most practical knowledge of the material world (the exterior and inferior lights) to the world of interiority (the interior light) and to the world of the sacred (the superior light). One senses here a movement similar to that found in the *Itinerarium*; from the world of exteriority, to the world of interiority, to the world of things above the soul. Also, the medieval hierarchical schema for relating the different sorts of beings encountered in the world appears here. If, in creating the world, God has signed it as a human artist signs a work of art, then the study of the world by humanity should involve, at some point, the detection of the divine signature. All creatures reflect God at least as vestiges. Higher on the hierarchy, some creatures reflect God as images. And when the image is filled with the reality of grace, it becomes a similitude. The signature of the divine Artist is present at every level of the hierarchy. As human beings organize their knowledge about the world into a variety of sciences, they are gathering fragments of that light which appears in its fullest form in theology.

#2. *Exterior light.*

Under the exterior light, Bonventure enumerates the seven mechanical arts. These include the basic arts and crafts by which human beings produce objects external to themselves. They are the ways in which human beings bring the external world to some sort of use for humanity, whether that be to serve fundamental human needs such as nourishment, clothing, and shelter, or for human enjoyment, such as music and theater. As Bonaventure indicates, the arts enable human beings to put things together for one of two reasons: utility or pleasure.

The mechanical arts enable human beings to moderate the forces of nature which seem, in so many ways, to be a threat to human survival. On this subject, Aristotle in his *Mechanica* says:

> Our wonder is excited, firstly, by phenomena which occur first in accordance with nature but of which we do not know the cause, and, secondly, by those which are produced by art despite nature for the benefit of humankind. Nature often operates contrary to human expediency, for she always follows the same course without deviation, whereas human expediency is always changing. When, therefore, we have to do something contrary to nature, the difficulty of it causes us perplexity and art has to be called to our aid. The kind of art which helps us in such perplexities we call Mechanical Skill. The words of the poet Antiphon are quite true: "Mastered by Nature, we o'ercome by Art."[7]

Living at a time when the medieval guilds were forming and the Crusades were giving impetus to the development of commerce, Hugh of St. Victor manifests a significant interest in such matters. This is reflected in his *Eruditio Didascalica*. Beyond the trivium and quadrivium of the liberal arts, Hugh lists seven mechanical arts: weaving, metal-working, architecture, agriculture, hunting, navigation, medicene, and dramatic art.[8] In the *De reductione*, Bonaventure follows Hugh's enumeration, but bases his classification simply on the purpose served by the arts: either utility or pleasure. Dramatic art is the only one in the second division; all the others supply people with the necessities of life.

At this point, these arts are simply named and described. In essence, they offer a description of the basic structures of medieval

---

[7] Cfr. *Works of Aristotle* translated under editorship of W.D. Ross, Oxford, 1931, Cfr. Ch. I, 847a.

[8] Lib. II, c. 21 (PL 176, 760).

life, beginning with the peasants working the fields and moving to the major guilds in which the craftsmen of the age were organized. From there, Bonaventure will take us also into the world of the scholars of the newly developed universities. How the mechanical arts are "led back" to theology will be discussed later in #11-14.

#3. *Inferior light.*

In this context, the term *inferior light* refers to the entire realm of sense knowledge by which we come to know natural forms. Sense perception is, as it were, the vestibule of intellectual knowledge. Through the sense faculties, the human person comes into contact with the material universe.

Theologians of the Middle Ages generally agreed that the soul is an indivisible, immaterial principle informing the body. This one single principle of life possesses a plurality of faculties and powers which Bonaventure reduces to three: the vegetative, the sensitive, and the rational. In the *Breviloquium* he describes these in the following way.

> The soul confers not only being but life, sensation, and intelligence. It therefore possesses a vegetative power, a power of sensation, and an intellectual power. By virtue of its vegetative power, the soul is the principle of gener-ation, nutrition, and growth. . . . By virtue of its sensitive power, the soul comprehends sensible objects, retains what it has apprehended, combines and sorts what it has retained. It apprehends through the five external senses that correspond to the five principal corporal elements of the world; it retains through memory; it combines and sorts through imagination, which is the primary collating power. Through its intellectual power, it discerns truth through reason, rejects evil through the irascible appetite, and desires good through the concupiscible appetite. Now, since the discernment of truth is cognitive, and since rejection and desire are affective, the soul as such is divided into the cognitive and the affective powers.[9]

The human subject, then, is situated as an embodied spirit in the universe of corporal realities; and human knowledge of the

---

[9] *Brevil.* 2, 9, 5 (V, 227).

world is acquired by interaction with the physical world, beginning with the impact that the physical realities have on the human subject and moving from there. This, of course, is a question of the action of the outside world on the sense organs of the human subject. Having no innate knowledge of beings in the empirical world, the rational human soul must gather its knowledge of material things through the senses. The soul, therefore, must be united with an appropriate sense apparatus. This is the human body. The organism, that is to say, the body "informed" by the soul is the seat of sensation. The sensible origin of our ideas about the external world is clearly recognized by the Seraphic Doctor.

"The light which enables us to discern natural forms," says Bonaventure, "is rightly called 'lower' because sense perception begins with a material object and takes place by the aid of corporal light." Here he brings to the fore the theory of light which we discussed above. The first form of matter is light. And the power of light extends to the lower operations of knowledge and brings from potency to act not only the sense of sight but all the other senses.[10]

Since there are five corporal substances in the world, namely the four elements and the form of light, the human subject is endowed with five senses. These are, as it were, the doors through which the sensible world may enter and impinge on human consciousness. In the third book of his *De Genesi ad litteram*,[11] Augustine shows that the earth corresponds to touch; water, to taste; air, to hearing; fire (warm vapor), to smell; the fifth essence, light, to sight. By the sense of sight, therefore, the soul comes into contact with luminous and colored bodies; by touch, with solid and terrestrial ones. The three intermediate senses afford a passage to the three intermediate elements: taste, to liquids; hearing, to air; smell, to the vapor resulting from a mixture of air, heat, and moisture.[12]

The mind acquires knowledge of a particular aspect of a particular thing. But the power of the mind is not limited to the formation of such percepts. As the above citation from the *Breviloquium* indicates, it is endowed with the additional power

---

[10] *II Sent.* 13, 3,2, (II, 328); *II Sent.* 13,1,3 (II, 379,381); *Brevil.* II, 3,2 (V, 220).

[11] C. 4, n.6 (PL 34, 281) and c. 16, n.32 (PL 34, 466).

[12] Cfr. *Itinerarium* 2,3 (V, 300).

of combining percepts and discriminating between one percept and another. Though the acts of the individual senses are distinct, there is in the mind the power to assemble the percepts resulting from these acts and to employ them for self-direction as effectively as if all the percepts were produced by a single sense. This is done by an interior sense faculty which is called the *common sense*.[13]

Every sense conveys information about the external world to the mind. This information reveals the fact that there are some objects in the world which are capable of imparting pleasure and other objects which are capable of causing pain. The formal objects of the senses are colored extension, sound, odor, taste, and extended pressure or resistance.[14] Sense pleasure is the satisfaction or repose which the faculties of a sentient being find in the possession or enjoyment of their proper objects. It is, therefore, an accompaniment of the natural, normal exercise of these faculties. If the stimulus is normal, the feeling is pleasant or agreeable. If the stimulus is abnormal, for example, a light or a sound that is too intense, the accompanying reaction is unpleasant and painful.[15] It is the internal or common sense which establishes these relations and combines the impressions that we experience.[16] The *reduction* of sense knowledge to theology is discussed in #8-10.

#4. *Interior light.*

The discussion of the interior light opens up the entire range of philosophical disciplines as known in the Middle Ages. Specifically, Bonaventure here describes philosophy as a science which guides the human person in the investigation of intelligible truth. Elsewhere he describes its distinctive character as the kind of certain knowledge which may be arrived at by means of investigation.[17] According to Hugh of St. Victor, this knowledge by means of the natural light of reason extends potentially to everything.[18]

---

[13] *IV Sent.* 50, 2, 1, 1, concl. (IV, 1045).
[14] *Itin.* 2, 3 (V, 390).
[15] *Itin.* 2, 5 (V, 301).
[16] *Itin.* 2, 6 (V, 301).
[17] *De donis S.S.*, 4, 6 (V, 474).
[18] *Eruditio Didascalica* 1,5 (PL 176, 744).

Bonaventure calls the light of philosophical knowledge *interior* because it inquires into the principles of knowledge and natural truth which are, in some way, connatural to the human mind.[19] It is Bonaventure's conviction that the truth which comes to light in the form of human knowledge rests finally in God, the Light in whom we see the unchangeable truth of things. There is, therefore, a *ratio* in the divine mind corresponding to everything that God knows or does. These archetypal forms, fixed and unchangeable and existing in the mind of God from all eternity, are called *Ideas*. They are perceived by human beings only by means of the inner eye of the intellect which God deems worthy of the things it strives to see. Considered as the principle of creation, the *Idea* is called an exemplar. As the principle of knowledge, the *Idea* is called a *ratio*, a *ratio intelligendi*, or a *ratio discernendi*.

Bonaventure refers to a controversy among the metaphysicians concerning the ideal reasons. This is very likely a reference to the difference between the Platonic and the Aristotelian views on the problem of the Ideas and the theory of exemplary causalilty. Aristotle rejected the Platonic view on both issues, and Bonaventure himself was critical of Aristotle precisely on these points, among others.

Bonaventure divides philosophical truth into three kinds which he calls rational philosophy, natural philosophy, and moral philosophy. The first, which might also be called the truth of thought or logical truth, studies the truth of concepts and words and the organization of these into judgments and statements. It is divided into logic, grammar, and rhetoric. The second is concerned with the truth of things, or with ontological truth. It is concerned with things in terms of their relation to the archetypes in the mind of God. This is divided into physics, mathematics, and metaphysics. And the third is concerned with the truth of human activity, or with the conformity of thought, word, and action in human life. In other words, it is knowledge brought to complete outward expression in the form of human activity. It is divided into individual ethics, family ethics, and social ethics.

---

[19] Beyond the text of the *De reductione* given here, cfr. also *De donis S.S.*, 4, 2 (V, 474).

The reduction of rational philosophy is found in #15-18; natural philosophy is found in #19-22; and moral philosophy is given in #23-25.

#5. *Superior light.*

This light is related to the truths of salvation. This is the light of the Scriptures or theology. This level of truth, in Bonaventure's understanding, lies beyond what reason can arrive at simply by studying the realities of the created order as such. This level has to do not with the nature of things as such, but with the final destiny of things which has been made known to us through the historical revelation embodied in the Scriptures. Thus, the starting point for the study of theology is to be found not in the data of reason but in the world of faith.[20]

As regards the manner of approaching the Scriptures, Bonaventure is abundantly clear and in line with most medieval thinking on the matter. Scripture, first of all, has a literal sense. Beyond this, it was customary to distinguish three levels or forms of spiritual interpretation; namely, the allegorical, the tropological, and the analogical. The allegorical interpretation is seen to refer principally to the development of the life of faith. The tropological is seen to relate to the moral life. And the anagogical is seen to hold the believer open in hope to the promise of a final reward.[21]

As regards the content of the Scriptures, Bonaventure reduces this to three basic points: (1) the eternal generation and incarnation of the Word or Son of God, (2) the pattern of human life, and (3) the goal of life which is loving union with God. It will be the task of the reduction to show how these three truths, which express the manifest wisdom of God, lie hidden in all knowledge and all nature (cfr. #26).

#6–7. The biblical creation account as found in the beginning of *Genesis* enters here with an analogical application of the six days of creation to the six branches of human knowledge into which the

---

[20] *De donis S.S.*, 4, 13 (V, 476).
[21] *Brevil.* prol. 4 (V, 205).

fourfold light has been divided. Corresponding to the first day on which God made light, which is the first form of all material realities, is the knowledge of Scripture. As light is the most noble substance in the natural order, so is the knowledge of Scripture the most elevated science in the hierarchy of human knowledge. As all material creation began with the light of the first day, so all the secular sciences or *artes* are related to the light of Scripture. They are contained in it and brought to perfection by it. As the six days of creation are followed by the seventh day of rest, so the six forms of knowledge will arrive at the Light of Glory where all historical forms of knowledge will be transcended.

The six days of creation help us to understand the line of argument in the *De reductione*. During this life, we have six ways of acquiring knowledge, namely, the six sciences or *lumina*, all of which come from the God of lights. The perfect number six[22] signifies the perfection of God s creation[23] and of human knowledge which finds its perfection in theology. This science of the supernatural order falls on the first day of the week and the light which it sheds is needed to walk the rest of the week, that is, the natural order of the *artes*. By walking in the light of the first day, we shall walk in the true light of faith and will ultimately attain to the eternal day, the great Sabbath which knows no evening.

Hence, Bonaventure insists that all knowledge must serve the understanding of the Scriptures and especially of the anagogical meaning, for through it the illumination is referred back to God whence it took its origin. Here Bonaventure appeals to a classical symbol of perfection, that of the circle. The circle of creation closes back on its beginning; the number six is complete; and thus, the movement of history is brought to rest. The Seraphic Doctor has set the stage. He is now ready to undertake the reduction he has promised.

---

[22] Six is a number which consists of the sum of its aliquot parts, i.e., of its sixth (=1), its third (=2) and its half (=3). An aliquot part is a part which divides a number exactly without remainder. Cfr. *II Sent.* 12, 1, 2, concl. (II,297); also, Augustine, *De genesi ad litt.*, 4, 21, 38ff (PL 34, 311).

[23] *II Sent.* 12, 1, 2 (II, 297).

III. *The reduction as such* (#8-25).

Bonaventure, as we have seen above, has described his entire metaphysics in terms of emanation, exemplarity, and consummation. As we will see in what follows, every argument of the *De reductione* reflects this line of thought. There is always a *point of departure* in the supreme Being; there is always the role of the *exemplar*; and the movement of thought takes us to the *return* that brings the creature back to its point of origin in a way that involves the fulfillment of the creature's potential. Bonaventure always preferred the Platonic doctrine of exemplarity over the more materialistic world-view of Aristotle and, indeed, saw the problem of exemplarity as the pre-eminent metaphysical question. But if the question emerges first as a philosophical question, its most adequate answer is to be found only in the person of Jesus Christ who is the historical incarnation of the primal Word in and through which God has created all that is created.

Several implications follow from this. First, a metaphysics that is ignorant of Christ runs the risk of being either incomplete or distorted and in need of correction. Second, something of what is most emphatically expressed in Christ may lie hidden in the great philosophical quests of those who had no knowledge of Christ, since all genuine truth somehow bears on Christ. This may be extended even to those who in fact are aware of Christ and share the Christian faith but have never thought out the implications of their faith. This may be a helpful way to look at the argument of the *De reductione*. The divine wisdom lies hidden in every form of secular knowledge. We need but to find the key to discover and unfold the appropriate analogies to allow that which is hidden to shine forth. As a result, each of the arts and sciences is made to bear on: (1) the eternal generation of the Word and his humanity; (2) the Christian order of life; and (3) the union of the soul with God.

A) *Sense perception led back to theology* (#8-10).

Already in the area of sense perception, Bonaventure finds hidden footprints which lead to God. In the consideration of the medium, the exercise, and the delight of sense perception, he sees an analogy to the eternal generation and incarnation of the Word, the pattern of human life, and the union of the soul with God.

Concerning the medium of perception, the issue is that of the way in which material objects project a likeness of themselves at a distance and thus reveal their presence and their nature provided that there is a sense organ available to receive the impression. It is by means of these forms or likenesses impressed first on the sense organ and leading eventually to a knowledge of the external object that we come to know the beings in the external world. This process involved in all sense experience reminds us of the Uncreated Light which generates its Likeness or Splendor, coequal, consubstantial, and co-eternal. If, then, all knowable objects have the power of generating their own likeness, they may be seen as mirrors in which the generation of the Word eternally emanating from God the Father is reflected; that very Word who became incarnate in Jesus Christ.

The exercise of sense perception alerts us to the pattern of human life. We have seen above that each sense relates only to its proper object, and that the senses try to avoid that which is imperfect or excessive in the object. We have seen also that there is a way in which the many sensations coming from the individual senses are coordinated by the internal senses, specifically by the common sense. The exercise of sense perception, therefore, is well-ordered and manifests a similar operation of the internal senses which operate in such a way as to reconstruct the image of the Word of God in the soul.

The internal senses are coordinated under the power of humility which is, in essence, a deep self-knowledge which opens to a new level of wisdom. Just as the external senses avoid an object which is unsuitable to them, so do the internal senses refrain from evil by the exercise of temperance. It is the role of this virtue to moderate the human drive for bodily delights in the use of food and drink, and in the use of what pertains to procreation. It is this virtue that enables us to prepare within ourselves a fit dwelling place for the Word.

Thus, from the orderly exercise of the external senses, we may learn something of the right order of the Christian life.

If we consider the delight involved in the orderly experience of sense objects, we will see something of the union of the soul with God. Each sense, in its own proper activity, finds the satisfaction of attaining its proper end; the enjoyment of sound, color, smell, etc. Similarly, the internal senses take delight in the contemplation of the good, the beautiful, etc. We can hear in this an echo of that joy which the soul will finally find in the fullness of its union with God for which it is created.

Now, all delight is at some level related to proportion.[24] Something of the classical, Greek canon of the aesthetic appears in Bonaventure's thought, mediated to him by the work of Augustine. Beauty is related to proportion; and proportion, in turn, is related to the Pythagorean understanding of number. This Greek tradition played a significant role in Augustine's *De musica*. There it is found together with the Platonic conviction that an object is beautiful to the degree that it approximates its original archetype. Bonaventure, following the lead of Augustine, gives this a trinitarian and christological interpretation. In terms of the trinity, he concludes that the supreme beauty is to be found in the Son because the Son is equal with the Father. Simply put, the Son is the *Ars Patris*. Hence, the second person of the trinity is the basis for all other beauty.

From here it becomes clear why it is that the likeness of sensible things, coming to the soul and delighting it with a certain beauty, sweetness, harmony, and fragrance alerts the soul to the first Image of God as the Fountain of all beauty and of everything that is agreeable to the human spirit. For in that first Image the most perfect harmony, proportion, and beauty is shared co-equally with the Father. So we move with Bonaventure from the delight of well-ordered sense experience to an awareness of the true and final delight which the human spirit will find in God. And if we look back over the way we have come, we see how the Wisdom of God lies hidden in sense experience, in terms of the likeness begotten by the object which makes sense experience possible, in terms of the orderly character of both the external and internal senses, and in terms of the delight in which sense experience culminates. The whole tells us of the generation and incarnation of the eternal

---

[24] *Itin.* 2, 5 (V, 300).

Word as likeness of the Father; of the well-ordered spiritual life; and of the end of both — the delight of the soul in union with God.

B) *Mechanical arts led back to theology* (#11-14).

The exterior light opens the entire world of the mechanical arts or the world of human workmanship or creativity. This form of human activity fairly begs for an analogical explication in relation to the one who is thought of as the Supreme Artisan, the Creator of all finite things.

Every work of art, as envisioned by Bonventure, is the external projection of a model or exemplar which exists in the mind of the artist. In this sense, a masterpiece of art exists in the mind of the artist before it is produced. If we think of the Creator God in an analogous way, then we would say that all creatures exist in the mind of God before they exist in their own right as realities external to God in the created world. In trinitarian terms, one would be led to say that from all eternity, the mind of God conceived a likeness of the divine itself thus giving expression to all that the divine is within itself, and all that it can bring into being outside itself. This divine self-expression is called at times the Word, at times the Image, at times the Son, and at times the Art of God.

The created cosmos, therefore, is the external projection of what is at first internal to God. The entire realm of creation, then, gives expression to something of the mystery of the divine. This takes place at different levels, depending on the degree to which the created copy approximates the divine original. Thus, in Bonaventure's view, every creature is at least a vestige of God. Another level is more "like" the original, and is called the image of God. And at yet another level, the image of God may become more intensely divinized by grace and is known as a similitude. We are looking at a hierarchically structured cosmos in which the place of each being in the cosmos is determined, at least in part, by the degree to which it reflects the mystery of the divine.

It is against this background that we are invited to think of the way in which a human artisan operates. Before actually producing a work of art, the artisan generates an interior image of what is to be produced outside. And as the external object is produced, the interior image remains within the mind of the artisan. Similarly, the inner, divine image remains within God when the external object is produced. And that external object is the whole of the universe.

Now the human artisan attempts to produce an external work as much like the interior image as possible. To such an extent, argues Bonaventure, that if it were possible to make an external image that was capable of knowing and loving the artisan, the artisan would do so. Such knowledge of the artisan could only be realized by virtue of the interior image which the artisan has of the external object. And if something should happen that would make it impossible for the external image to know the internal image, this could be overcome if the internal image, while remaining within the mind of the artisan, made itself visible externally.

With this in mind, Bonaventure recalls how humanity was created as an image of God, and in the state of Paradise, capable not of the beatific vision of God but of a form of knowledge between that which we have of God in this world and that which we will have in heaven. Our first parents saw God in the light of contemplation. This was lost with sin, and humanity became blinded. For this reason the eternal and invisible Word took on flesh in order to lead us back to God. Thus, we can see the rationale of the incarnation of the eternal Word who, while remaining internal to the divine mind, became visible in the form of Jesus of Nazareth to lead us back to God. And so it is that in the production of every work of art there is contained an analogy to the Son of God, begotten from all eternity and incarnate in the fulness of time.

Bonaventure now looks at the work of art itself, which he says should be beautiful, useful, and enduring. Like a work of art, human life should have three similar qualities. Thus, he is concerned with showing how the virtues of the Christian *ordo vivendi* reflect such qualities. Here he appeals to Aristotle's three requisites for virtue and shows that they can make our spiritual workmanship beautiful, useful, and enduring. "We must understand, will, and unceasingly toil."[25]

---

[25] Cfr. Aristotle, *II Ethic.* c. 4 and *X Ethic.* c. 9.

In speaking of the fruit of the artisan's efforts beyond that of the actual work of art, Bonaventure refers to three appetitive qualities. He thus shows the similarity between the fruit of physical and spiritual workmanship. In the production of a work of art, he says, every artisan seeks praise, advantage, or delight — three aims which correspond to the *bonum honestum, conferens, et delectabile*. God's purpose in endowing humanity with a rational soul was that humanity might recognize in the Creator a *bonum honestum, conferens et delectabile* and thereby come to praise God, serve God, find delight in God, and be at rest. There is within the human heart an innate longing for happiness. But the existence of such a desire would be absurd if its satisfaction were not possible. This satisfaction is attained only by the possession of the highest and ultimate end, the Supreme Good.[26] The sole end in which the human will finds its complete satisfaction is Uncreated Love, that is God. Our end, then, is to enjoy God; it is by charity that we love God. Charity, therefore, constitutes our end.[27] Our end, then, is a loving union with God through which the human being is transformed into the highest God-likeness.

From all of the foregoing, we see how the divine Wisdom lies hidden in the knowledge of the mechanical arts.

C) *Rational philosophy led back to theology* (#15-18).

In a similar way, divine Wisdom can be found in the light of rational philosophy. Here Bonaventure is concerned with language in terms of the speaker, the delivery of speech, and the goal or the hearer of speech.

The trinitarian background for Bonaventure's discussion is clear. The primary metaphor is that of the inner word and the external word. The inner Word in God is the second person of the trinity. The outer word is, first of all, creation; and more specifically, humanity. The pre-eminent instance of the external expression of the inner divine Word is found in the incarnation where the divine Word assumes the reality of human flesh.

---

[26] *Itin.* 3, 4 (V, 305).
[27] *II Sent.* 38, 1, 2, fund. 3 (II, 883).

The inner word in human beings is the word of consciousness. From out of the well of consciousness, the intellect generates thoughts or internal words. These inner words find expression externally in the form of language and speech. The analogy with the trinity and the incarnation is clear. As the inner word of the mind takes the form of the voice that it may be known to other intelligent beings, and still does not depart from the mind of the person conceiving it, so did the Eternal Word assume flesh and dwell among us so as to become known to human beings. And yet the same Word remained internal to God as God's immanent self-expression.[28]

Turning to the actual delivery of speech, Bonaventure singles out three qualities of human speech: fittingness, truth, and style. These parallel three qualities that should characterize our moral life: namely, measure, beauty, and, order. These, in turn, are related to modesty, purity of affection, and uprightness of intention. It is in the harmonious blending of these three characteristics that Bonaventure finds the pattern of a Christian life. Thus, we can see an analogy between the delivery of speech and the well-ordered human life which is the concern of revelation.

The purpose of speech, says Bonaventure, is to express a thought, to teach, and to persuade. He here appeals to the Augustinian tradition of the "inner teacher" to argue that this threefold purpose of speech cannot be accomplished unless the human speaker be united with the divine source of truth, namely, with Christ, the "inner teacher."[29] Thus, the purpose of speech implies a goal which has a certain analogy with the final goal of human life; union with God.

D) *Natural philosophy led back to theology* (#19-22).

It is the same form of reasoning that leads natural philosophy to theology. Natural philosophy, for Bonaventure, is concerned with the formal causes of things. These formal causes exist at three

---

[28] *In Nativitate Domini, Sermo II* (IX, 107). For translation and commentary, cfr. Z. Hayes, *What Manner of Man? Sermons on Christ by St. Bonaventure* (Chicago, 1974) 57ff.

[29] Augustine, *De Magistro*, 1, 11, 38 (PL, 32, 1216); Bonaventure, *Sermo IV, Christus unus omnium magister*, 1 (V, 567); for translation and commentary, cfr. Hayes, *op. cit.*, 21ff.

levels: in material beings themselves, in the human mind, and in the divine mind. These may be called also the seminal forms, the intellectual or abstract forms, and the ideal forms.

The many material beings of nature are the result of the development of seminal principles with which God endowed matter from the beginning, an idea which can be traced back to St. Augustine. These seminal principles are, as it were, active forces in matter or principles of growth and development. And wherever these forms are present and operative in reality, they prepare matter to receive other forms. Thus, matter first receives the form of the elements. In this way it becomes capable of receiving the form of an organic compound. Then, out of the intermediate forms of an organic substance through the mediation of light there arises the form of an organic body in which the seminal principle attains its full development. Thus, by a series of progressive changes, nature attains its perfect form, the higher form in matter developing when the lower form has brought matter to the degree of organization which would permit its further development.

Not only is there generation and productivity in matter, but the intellectual forms flow out of the inner word of the mind by means of intellectual generation. Looking at both of these, the seminal forms and the intellectual forms, Bonaventure concludes that "if such productivity characterizes the creature, with greater reason should we expect to find it in the Creator" in Whom exist the ideal principles of all things.[30] Thus, the divine mind expresses by a wholly internal act the Word of divine self-expression which is the perfect reproduction of the divinity itself. It is for this reason called the *ars omnipotentis Dei* by Augustine.[31] Now this divine self-image would not be a complete image unless it represented not only the infinite being of God but also all the possible ways in which God can and will communicate being outside the divinity itself. So the Word is both the representation of God and the model or Exemplar of all created things as well.[32]

From another perspective, Bonaventure argues that the perfection of the universe cannot be attained as long as the appetite

---

[30] *I Sent.* 9, 1, (I, 181).
[31] *De trinitate VI*, 10, 11 (PL 42, 931).
[32] *Hex.* 1, 13 (V, 331).

for form which lies within matter does not result in the union of a material body with a rational soul. This would be the fulfillment of the desire of matter for its ultimate form. Body and soul, argues Bonaventure, do not stand in neutral juxtaposition next to each other. Rather, each has an active desire for union with the other. When they come together in the form of a human being, this form of being contains both the seminal principles and the intellectual principles.

But even here the highest perfection of the universe would be lacking, for still more is possible. It is only when a nature containing the seminal principles and a nature containing the intellectual principles are united in one person with that nature which contains the ideal principles that the fullest perfection of the universe is realized. Thus in paragraph #20, Bonaventure offers what may well be seen as a very succinct statement of the central insight of a cosmic christology. What has happened between God and the world in Christ is the fulfillment of the deepest potential of the created cosmos so that a cosmos without Christ would not have reached its fullness.

In discussing the question of causality, Bonaventure sees something of the pattern of Christian life. To understand his argument one must recall the physics, and specifically, the role of light in his understanding of the physical cosmos which we discussed briefly above. Generation by seminal causes takes place through the beneficent light of the heavenly bodies. The sun is the highest of the heavenly bodies. From its place in the heavens it gives light to the moon and the stars. By its life-giving heat, it makes the plants, seeds, and trees live and blossom. Its power extends even beneath the earth where it produces the metals. "By reason of the pressure, movement, and union of elements caused by their power and heat, the heavenly bodies aid in the production of minerals, vegetables, animals, and the human body."[33]

This relation of the heavenly bodies to all the material processes provides a useful metaphor for the relation of Christ, Mary, and the other saints to the life of the human soul. Christ is the light of the soul who by his grace awakens the seminal principles of the virtues dormant in it and enables them to bear

---

[33] *Brevil.* 4, 1 (V, 241); and *Itin.* 2, 2 (V, 300).

their fruits. As the sun, the highest of the heavenly bodies, rules the day with splendor; as the moon rules the night by reflected light; and as the stars adorn the heavens; so too, the soul, if it is to live and operate in grace, must receive from Christ the light of infused grace, live under the protection of Mary, and imitate the virtues of the saints.

And if we consider the medium of the union in formal causes, we shall see there the union of the soul with God. As a plant can germinate and grow only if air, heat, and rain penetrate the soil; and as the body receives life from the soul only by means of the moisture, warmth, and vital energy or breath of life, so the soul can be united with God only when similar life-giving elements are present at the level of the spiritual life.

E) *Moral philosophy led back to theology* (#23-25).

Moral philosophy, which deals principally with rectitude or justice, also can be seen in relation to theology. The entire discussion involves a certain play on the Latin noun *rectitudo* and the related adjective *rectus*. The Latin word *rectus* means simply *straight* or *upright*. This can be a geometric description. It can also be used with a certain ethical or moral weight. This becomes clear in Bonaventure's discussion of three definitions which can be given to the word *right*. For the first definition, he refers to a text of Plato.[34] The primary meaning here is geometrical. It depends on the proper description of a straight line. A line is said to be straight if its mid-point is in perfect alignment with its two extreme points. This then becomes a metaphor for the divine *straightness* or *rectitude* which, in turn, will be a metaphor for the trinitarian life. If in God there is Beginning and End, then it is fitting that there be a mid-point in the line between Beginning and End, or a middle person in the life of the trinity. The idea of a middle person had been part of Bonaventure's trinitarian theology from early in his career. It is part of the way in which he appropriated the vision of Richard of St. Victor into his own systematic trinitarianism. But the person who stands at the center

---

[34] Cfr. *II Sent.*, prooem., note 11 (II, 4). The Quaracchi editors refer to Plato in *Parmenides*. The Latin given by the editors is: Rectum vero illud, cuius medium extremis utrisque e regione est.

of the trinity —the Son, or the Word —is also the intermediary by means of whom God reaches out as Creator of the universe. The same eternal middle person is the one who would become incarnate in time so as to serve as the mediator needed to lead creation back to God. Thus, the question of *rectitude* which is the primary concern of moral philosophy opens us to the vision of the eternal generation of the Son and the incarnation of the Son in time.

But, in another sense, the word *right* describes something that is in conformity with the norm by which it is measured. For human beings, perfect rectitude requires conformity with the will of God. It was necessary, therefore, that the divine will be made known. God gave a threefold sign of the divine will in the commandments, the prohibitions, and counsels. Thus, when moral philosophy is viewed from this perspective, it stands in analogy with the revealed pattern of life which is the concern of theology.

In the case of the third definition of *right*, "something is called right when its summit is raised upward." Here it would be useful to refer to Bonaventure's understanding of the text of *Ecclesiastes* 7:30: "God made humankind upright."[35] Here Bonaventure takes this to mean "standing upright" with feet on the ground and the head at the highest point. But beyond this, a human being is genuinely upright when the intellect is in harmony with the divine truth; the will is in harmony with the divine good; and the dominating power is in harmony with the loving creative power of God. When this is the case, the human being will not only be *right*, but will also be *ruler* and *king*. Here Bonaventure engages in yet another play on words: *rectus/rector/rex*. This may be seen as the ideal description of humanity as Bonaventure sees things. Unfortunately, it is not humankind as we find ourselves empirically in history. Borrowing another metaphor from Scripture, Bonaventure says that instead of standing upright as just described, we go through life bent over and incapable of seeing. This is the issue of sin and the distortions it has brought with it.

This background from the earlier writings of Bonaventure can be heard echoing through the present text. In this case, the upright posture of the human person with head at the top stands as a symbol of the final destiny of humanity: loving union with God.

---

[35] *II Sent.* prooem. (II, 3ff).

Since God transcends any human possibility, it is necessary that the high-point of the human person (=*apex mentis*), here symbolized by the head at the summit of the upright human being, be brought into union with the mystery of the God that transcends it and draws the human spirit above itself. Only when all the human, spiritual powers are in alignment with the divine truth, goodness, and power can the human person be said to be fully *upright*. So it is that the third definition of *rectitude* elicits an awarness of the final end of humanity which is the concern of theology.

IV. *Conclusion* (#26).

One cannot read Bonaventure for long without being deeply impressed by his exceptional power of synthesis. The case of the present text is an outstanding example. There is hardly a line or even a word in this text that appears superfluous. And the whole is shaped by theological convictions which have been hammered out over many years. These are primarily of a trinitarian and a christological sort. If one takes into account his convictions concerning these premises and their relation to exemplaristic metaphysics, the central logic of this work becomes clear. And it is worked out here with remarkble consistency and coherence. These are the marks of the skillful systematic theologian.

Bonventure brings his work to a resounding conclusion with an epilogue that might well be seen as a charter for Christian spirituality and education. Everything that pertains to the world of God's creation is drawn into this remarkable vision. Nothing is left behind. All is taken up into the journey of the human spirit to deeper wisdom and into ever richer, loving union with the mystery of God whose goodness, truth, and beauty have been so richly poured out on the created world. The pursuit of knowledge and the cultivation of the intellectual life is not a goal in itself, but is best seen as a dimension of the human journey into God. It is in this sense that theology is described as a practical science.

In the first of his *Collations on the Hexaemeron*, Bonaventure shows in considerable detail how Christ is the center of all things.[36] The one who is from all eternity the central person of the trinity assumes flesh and becomes the center of the created world and its history. Through his life, death, and resurrection the created world has been restored to a wholeness lost by the Fall of Adam. The eternal Word is the principle through whom God creates all things. The incarnate Word is the Mediator through whom human beings are united to God in grace. The inspired Word is the principle by which we arrive at Christian wisdom, for in Christ are contained all the treasures of wisdom and knowledge. Whoever desires to return to God must return by and through the mystery of Christ.

Viewed from this perspective, the *De reductione* is the most compact statement of Bonaventure's vision to be found in the entire body of his writings. It is pre-eminently a wisdom-theology. By this we mean that it unfolds a way not only of knowing but above all a way of living out the fullness of the human, spiritual journey into God. All knowledge and speculation is put into the service of the final goal of human life; namely, a transforming, mystical union with the mystery of divine love.

We can read the *De reductione* as the answer to the third question of Bonaventure's metaphysics: How do things return to God?[37] All along the journey, the Seraphic Doctor has discovered signals of that divine wisdom that lies hidden in all of nature, in every human sense experience, and in every form of human knowledge. By thus aligning all the human sciences in relation to the final goal of human life as revealed in the Scriptures, Bonaventure has provided a firm basis for describing the goal of all knowledge and intellectual culture in the following words: "that faith may be strengthened, God may be honored, character may be formed, and consolation may be derived from union of the Spouse with the beloved, a union which takes place through charity. . . . a charity without which all knowledge is vain."

---

[36] *Hex.* 1 (V, 329-335).

[37] *Hex.* 1, 17 (V, 332)

The Latin Text
"De reductione artium ad theologiam"

The Text in Translation
On the Reduction of the Arts to Theology

De Reductione Artium ad Theologiam

1. *Omne datum optimum et omne donum perfectum desursum est, descendens a Patre luminum,* Iacobus in Epistolae suae primo capitulo. In hoc verbo tangitur origo omnis illuminationis, et simul cum hoc insinuatur multiplicis luminis ab illa fontali luce liberalis emanatio. Licet autem omnis illuminatio cognitionis interna sit, possumus tamen rationabiliter distinguere, ut dicamus, quod est lumen *exterius,* scilicet lumen artis mechanicae; lumen *inferius,* scilicet lumen cognitionis sensitivae; lumen *interius,* scilicet lumen cognitionis philosophicae; lumen *superius,* scilicet lumen gratiae et sacrae Scripturae. Primum lumen illuminat respectu figurae *artificialis,* secundum respectu *formae naturalis,* tertium respectu *veritatis intellectualis,* quartum et ultimum respectu *veritatis salutaris.*

2. Primum igitur lumen, quod illuminat ad figuras *artificiales,* quae quasi exterius sunt et propter supplendam corporis indigentiam repertae, dicitur lumen *artis mechanicae;* quae, quia quodam modo servilis est et degenerat a cognitione philosophiae, recte potest dici *exterius.* Et illud septuplicatur secundum septem artes mechanicas, quas assignat Hugo in Didascalico, quae sunt scilicet lanificium, armatura, agricultura, venatio, navigatio, medicina, theatrica. — Quarum *sufficientia* sic accipitur. Quoniam omnis ars mechanica aut est ad *solatium,* aut ad *commodum;* sive aut est ad excludendam *tristitiam,* aut *indigentiam;* sive aut *prodest,* aut *delectat,* secundum illud Horatii:

Aut prodesse volunt, aut delectare poetae.

Et iterum:

Omne tulit punctum qui miscuit utile dulci.

Si est ad *solatium* et delectationem, sic est *theatrica,* quae est ars ludorum, omnem modum ludendi continens, sive sit in cantibus, sive in organis, sive in figmentis, sive in gesticulationibus corporis. — Si vero ordinatur

On the Reduction of the Arts to Theology

1. *Every good gift and every perfect gift is from above, coming down from the God of Lights,* writes James in the first chapter of his epistle. This text speaks of the source of all illumination; but at the same time, it suggests that there are many lights which flow generously from that fontal source of light. Even though every illumination of knowledge is internal, still we can reasonably distinguish what may be called an *exterior* light, or the light of mechanical art; an *inferior* light, or the light of sense perception; an *interior* light, or the light of philosophical knowledge; and a *superior* light, or the light of grace and of Sacred Scripture. The first light illumines with respect to the forms of *artifacts*; the second, with respect to *natural forms*; the third, with respect to *intellectual truth*; the fourth and last, with respect to *saving truth*.

2. So the first light, which sheds its light on the forms of *artifacts* — things which are, as it were, external to the human person and intended to supply the needs of the body — is called the light of *mechanical art.* Since this is, in a certain sense, servile and of a lower nature than philosophical knowledge, this light can rightly be called *exterior.* It is divided into seven, corresponding to the seven mechanical arts listed by Hugh in his *Didascalicon,* namely, weaving, armour–making, agriculture, hunting, navigation, medicine, and the dramatic art. That the above–mentioned arts *are sufficient* is shown in the following way. Every mechanical art is intended either for our *consolation* or for our *comfort*; its purpose, therefore, is to banish either *sorrow* or *need*; it is either *useful* or *enjoyable,* according to the words of Horace:

Poets desire either to be useful or to please.

And again:

One who combines the useful with the delightful wins universal applause.

If its purpose is to afford *consolation* and delight, it is *dramatic art,* or the art of producing plays. This embraces every form of entertainment, including song, instrumental music, poetry, or pantomime. If, how-

ad *commodum* sive profectum secundum exteriorem hominem, hoc potest esse aut quantum ad *operimentum,* aut quantum ad *alimentum,* aut quantum ad *utriusque adminiculum.* — Si quantum ad *operimentum,* aut illud est de materia molli et leni, sic est *lanificium;* aut de materia dura et forti, et sic est *armatura* sive ars fabrilis, quae continet omnem armaturam fabricatam sive ex ferro, sive ex quocumque metallo, sive lapide, sive ligno.

Si vero iuvat quantum ad *cibum,* hoc potest esse dupliciter: quia cibamur *vegetabilibus,* aut *sensibilibus.* Si quantum ad *vegetabilia,* sic est *agricultura;* si quantum ad *sensibilia,* sic est *venatio.* Vel aliter: si iuvat quantum ad *cibum,* hoc potest esse dupliciter: aut iuvat quantum ad ciborum *genituram* et multiplicationem, et tunc est agricultura; aut quantum ad cibi multiplicem *praeparationem,* et sic est venatio, quae continet omne genus praeparandi cibos et potus et sapores, quod pertinet ad pistores, coquos et caupones. Denominatur autem ab unius parte solum propter quandam excellentiam et curialitatem.

Si autem est in *utriusque adminiculum,* hoc est dupliciter: aut *defectum supplendo,* et sic est *navigatio,* sub qua continetur omnis *mercatio* sive pertinentium ad operimentum, sive ad alimentum; aut *removendo impedimentum* et nocumentum, et sic est *medicina,* sive consistat in confectione electuariorum, sive potionum, sive unguentorum, sive curatione vulnerum, sive decisione membrorum, sicut est chirurgia. —Theatrica autem est unica. Et sic patet sufficientia.

3. Secundum lumen, quod illuminat nos ad *formas naturales* apprehendendas, est lumen *cognitionis sensitivae,* quod recte dicitur *inferius,* quia cognitio sensitiva ab inferiori incipit et fit beneficio lucis corporalis. Et hoc quintuplicatur secundum quinque sensus. — Quorum *sufficientiam* sumit Augustinus secundum naturam luminis elementorum in tertio super Genesi hoc modo: quia lumen sive lux faciens ad distinctionem rerum corporearum aut est in suae *proprietatis eminentia* et quadam puritate, et sic est sensus *visus,* aut *commiscetur aëri,* et sic est *auditus,* aut *vapori* et sic est *odoratus* aut *humori,* et sic est

ever, it is intended for the *comfort* or betterment of the outer person, it can accomplish its purpose by providing either *shelter* or food, or by helping *in the acquisition of either.* If it is a matter of *shelter,* it will be concerned either with something of a soft and light material, in which case it is *weaving;* or with something of a strong and hard material, in which case it is *armour–making* or metal–working, an art which includes the production of every instrument made of iron or of any other metal, or of stone or wood.

If a mechanical art is helpful with respect to food, this can be in two ways, for we take our nourishment from *vegetables* and from *animals.* If it is concerned with *vegetables,* it is *farming;* if it is concerned with *animals,* it is *hunting.* Or again, a mechanical art can be useful in two ways with respect to food. Either it can aid in the *production* and multiplication of crops, in which case it is agriculture; or it can aid in the various ways of *preparing* food. Viewed in this way, it is hunting, an art which includes every conceivable way of preparing foods, drinks, and delicacies. This is the task of bakers, cooks, and innkeepers. It is named from only one of these activities, and that because of its nobility and courtly character.

If it is an aid in acquiring either shelter or food, this may be in two ways. Either it *serves to fill a need,* in which case it is *navigation,* an art which includes all forms of *commerce* in articles intended for shelter or for food; or it serves by *removing impediments* and ills of the body, in which case it is *medicine,* whether it is concerned with the preparation of drugs, potions, or ointments, with the healing of wounds, or with the amputation of members. In this latter case it is called surgery. Dramatic art, on the other hand, is the only one of its kind. Thus the sufficiency (of the mechanical arts) is evident.

3. The second light, which provides light for the apprehension of *natural forms,* is the light of *sense knowledge.* This is rightly called the *inferior* light because sense perception begins with an inferior object and takes place by the aid of corporal light. It has five divisions corresponding to the five senses. In the third book of his work *On Genesis,* Saint Augustine bases the *adequacy* of the senses on the nature of the light present in the elements in the following way. If the light or brightness which is responsible for the distinction of corporal things exists in its own *perfection* and in a *certain purity,* this pertains to the sense of

gustus; aut *terrae grossitiei,* et sic est *tactus.* Spiritus enim sensibilis naturam luminis habet, unde in nervis viget, quorum natura est clara et pervia; et in istis quinque sensibus multiplicatur secundum maiorem et minorem depurationem. Itaque cum quinque sint corpora mundi simplicia, scilicet quatuor elementa et quinta essentia; ut homo omnes formas corporeas posset percipere, quinque sensus habet illis correspondentes; quia nulla fit apprehensio nisi per aliquam similitudinem et convenientiam organi et obiecti, pro eo quod sensus est natura determinata. Est et alius modus sumendi sufficientiam sensuum, sed hunc approbat Augustinus, et rationabilis videtur, quia ad hanc sufficientiam simul concurrunt correspondentia ex parte organi, medii et obiecti.

4. Tertium lumen, quod illuminat ad *veritates intelligibiles* perscrutandas, est lumen *cognitionis philosophicae,* quod ideo *interius* dicitur, quia interiores causas et latentes inquirit, et hoc per principia disciplinarum et veritatis naturalis, quae homini naturaliter sunt inserta. Et hoc triplicatur in *rationalem, naturalem, et moralem.* — Et sufficientia potest accipi sic. Est enim veritas *sermonum,* veritas *rerum* et veritas *morum. Rationalis* veritatem *sermonum* considerat, *naturalis* veritatem *rerum, moralis* veritatem, *morum.* — Vel aliter: sicut in summo Deo est considerare rationem causae efficientis, formalis sive exemplaris, et finalis, quia "est causa subsistendi, ratio intelligendi et ordo vivendi;" sic in ipsa illuminatione philosophiae, quoniam illuminat aut ad cognoscendas *causas essendi,* et sic est *physica;* aut *rationes intelligendi,* et sic *est logica;* aut *ordinem vivendi,* et sic est *moralis* sive practica. Tertio modo sic: quia lumen cognitionis philosophicae illuminat ipsam intellectivam; hoc autem potest esse tripliciter: aut in quantum regit *motivam,* et sic est *moralis;* aut in quantum regit *se ipsam,* et sic est *naturalis;* aut in quantum regit *interpretativam,* et sic est *sermocinalis;* ut sic illuminetur homo ad veritatem vitae, ad veritatem scientiae et ad veritatem doctrinae.

sight; if it is *mixed with the air,* it pertains to *hearing;* if *with vapor,* it pertains to smell; if *with fluid,* it pertains to *taste;* if *with the solidity of earth,* it pertains to *touch.* Now since the sensitive spirit partakes of the nature of light, it thrives in the nerves, whose nature it is to be clear and penetrable; and this light is received in these five senses according to the greater or lesser degree of its purity. And so, since there are five simple corporal substances in the world, namely, the four elements and the fifth essence, the human person has five senses that correspond to these so that the person might be able to perceive all bodily forms; since, because of the well-defined nature of each sense, no apprehension would be possible without a certain similarity and correspondence between the sense-organ and the object. There is another way of determining the adequacy of the senses, but Augustine approves this method; and it seems reasonable, because of the simultaneous correspondence of the elements on the part of the organ, the medium, and the object.

4. The third light, which enlightens the human person in the investigation of *intelligible truths,* is the light of *philosophical knowledge.* It is called *interior* because it inquires into inner and hidden causes through principles of learning and natural truth, which are connatural to the human mind. There is a threefold division of this light into *rational, natural,* and *moral* philosophy. That this is sufficient can be understood in the following way. There is the truth of *speech,* the truth of *things,* and the truth of *morals. Rational* philosophy considers the truth of *speech; natural* philosophy, the truth of *things;* and *moral* philosophy, the truth of *conduct.* We may look at this in a different way. Just as we find in the most high God efficient, formal or exemplary, and final causality, since "God is the cause of being, the principle of intelligibility, and the order of human life," so we may find these in the illumination of philosophy, which enlightens the mind to discern the *causes of being,* in which case it is *physics;* or to know the *principles of understanding,* in which case it is *logic;* or to learn the *order of living,* in which case it is *moral* or practical philosophy. This issue may be viewed in yet a third way. The light of philosophical knowledge illumines the intellect itself and this enlightenment may be threefold: if it directs the *motive power,* it is *moral* philosophy; if it *directs itself,* it is *natural* philosophy; if it directs *the interpretive power,* it is *discursive* philosophy. As a result, hu-

Et quoniam tripliciter potest aliquis per *sermonem* exprimere quod habet apud se, ut scilicet notum faciat mentis suae conceptum, vel ut amplius moveat ad credendum, vel ut moveat ad amorem, vel odium: ideo *sermocinalis* sive rationalis philosophia triplicatur, scilicet in *grammaticam, logicam* et *rhetoricam;* quarum prima est ad exprimendum, secunda ad docendum, tertia ad movendum. Prima respicit rationem ut *apprehensivam;* secunda, ut *iudicativam;* tertia, ut *motivam.* Et quia ratio apprehendit per sermonem *congruum,* iudicat per *verum,* movet per sermonem *ornatum:* hinc est, quod haec triplex scientia has tres passiones circa sermonem considerat.

    Rursus, quoniam intellectus noster dirigi habet in iudicando secundum rationes formales, et hae tripliciter possunt considerari: vel in comparatione ad *materiam,* et sic dicuntur *rationes formales;* vel in comparatione ad *animam,* et sic *intellectuales;* vel in comparatione ad *divinam sapientiam,* et sic *ideales:* ideo *naturalis* philosophia triplicatur in *physicam proprie dictam,* in *mathematicam* et in *metaphysicam;* ita quod *physica* consideratio est circa rerum generationem et corruptionem secundum virtutes naturales et rationes seminales; *mathematica* est circa considerationem formarum abstrahibilium secundum rationes intelligibiles; *metaphysica,* circa cognitionem omnium entium, quae reducit ad unum primum principium, a quo exierunt secundum *rationes ideales,* sive ad Deum in quantum *principium finis,* et *exemplar;* licet inter metaphysicos de huiusmodi rationibus idealibus nonnulla fuerit controversia.

    Postremo, quia regimen virtutis *motivae* tripliciter habet attendi, scilicet respectu *vitae propriae,* respectu *familiae* et respectu *multitudinis subiectae;* ideo *moralis* philosophia triplicatur, scilicet in *monasticam, oeconomicam* et *politicam;* quae distinguuntur secundum triplicem modum praedictum, sicut apparet ex ipsis nominibus.

    5. Quartum autem lumen, quod illuminat ad *veritatem salutarem,* est lumen *sacrae Scripturae,* quod ideo dicitur *superius,* quia ad superiora ducit manifestando quae sunt supra rationem, et etiam quia non per inventionem, sed per inspirationem a *Patre luminum* descendit. Quod licet *unum* sit secundum intelle*ctum litteralem,* est

manity is enlightened as regards the truth of life, the truth of knowledge, and the truth of doctrine.

Since there are three reasons why one might express through speech what one has in mind: namely, to reveal one's thought, to move another to greater faith, or to arouse love or hatred in another, it follows that *discursive* or rational philosophy has three sub–divisions: *grammar, logic,* and *rhetoric.* Of these sciences the first is concerned with expressing; the second with teaching; the third with persuading. The first considers reason as *apprehending;* the second, as *judging;* the third, as *persuading.* Since reason apprehends through *appropriate* speech, judges through *true* speech, and persuades through *eloquent* speech, it is appropriate that these three sciences consider these three qualities in speech.

Again, since our intellect must be guided by formal principles in making a judgment, these principles, in turn, can be viewed from three perspectives: in relation to *matter,* they are called *formal;* in relation to the *mind,* they are called *intellectual;* and in relation to *divine wisdom,* they are called *ideal.* Therefore *natural* philosophy is subdivided into *physics* in the proper sense, *mathematics,* and *metaphysics.* So it is that *physics* treats of the generation and corruption of things according to natural powers and seminal principles; *mathematics* considers abstract forms in terms of their intelligible causes; *metaphysics* is concerned with the knowledge of all beings according to their *ideal causes,* tracing them back to the one first Principle from which they proceeded, that is, to God, in as far as God is the *Beginning,* the *End,* and the *Exemplar.* However, there has been some controversy among the metaphysicians concerning these ideal causes.

Since the direction of the motive power is to be considered in a threefold way, namely, as regards the *life of the individual,* the *family,* and the *state,* so there is a threefold division of *moral* philosophy corresponding to this: namely, *personal, domestic,* and *political,* the meaning of which is clear from the very names used to designate them.

5. Now the fourth light, which provides illumination with respect to *saving truth,* is the light of *sacred Scripture.* This light is called *superior* because it leads to higher things by revealing truths which transcend reason, and also because it is not acquired by human research, but comes down from the *"God of Lights"* by inspiration. While

tamen *triplex* secundum sensum *mysticum* et spiritualem. In omnibus enim sacrae Scripturae libris praeter *litteralem* sensum, quem exterius verba sonant, concipitur triplex sensus *spiritualis*, scilicet *allegoricus*, quo docemur, quid sit credendum de Divinitate et humanitate; *moralis*, quo docemur, quomodo vivendum sit; et *anagogicus*, quo docemur qualiter est Deo adhaerendum. Unde tota sacra Scriptura haec tria docet, scilicet Christi aeternam generationem et incarnationem, vivendi ordinem et Dei et animae unionem. Primum respicit *fidem*, secundum *mores*, tertium *finem utriusque*. Circa primum insudare debet studium doctorum, circa secundum studium praedicatorum, circa tertium studium contemplativorum. Primum maxime docet Augustinus, secundum maxime docet Gregorius, tertius vero docet Dionysius Anselmus sequitur Augustinum, Bernardus sequitur Gregorium, Richardus sequitur Dionysium, quia Anselmus in ratiocinatione, Bernardus in praedicatione, Richardus in contemplatione; Hugo vero omnia haec.

6. Ex praedictis colligitur, quod licet ex primaria divisione *quadruplex* sit lumen desursum descendens; sunt tamen *sex* eius differentiae: scilicet lumen *sacrae Scripturae*, lumen *cognitionis sensitivae*, lumen *artis mechanicae*, lumen *philosophiae rationalis*, lumen *philosophiae naturalis* et lumen *philosophiae moralis*. Et ideo sex illuminationes sunt in vita ista et habent vesperam, quia omnis *scientia destruetur*; et ideo succedit eis septima dies requietionis, quae vesperam non habet, scilicet *illuminatio gloriae*.

7. Unde valde apte possunt reduci sex istae illuminationes ad senarium formationum sive illuminationum, in quibus factus est mundus, ut cognitio sacrae Scripturae primae formationi, scilicet formationi lucis, respondeat; et sic deinceps per ordinem. — Et sicut omnes illae ab una luce habebant originem, sic omnes istae cognitiones ad cognitionem sacrae Scripturae ordinantur, in ea clauduntur et in illa perficiuntur, et mediante illa ad aeternam illuminationem ordinantur. Unde omnis nostra cognitio in cognitione sacrae Scripturae debet habere statum, et maxime quantum ad intellectum *anagogiae*, per

in its *literal* sense it is *one*, still, in its spiritual and *mystical* sense, it is *threefold*, for in all the books of sacred Scripture, beyond the *literal* meaning which the words express outwardly, there is a threefold *spiritual* meaning: namely, the *allegorical*, by which we are taught what to believe concerning the divinity and humanity; the *moral*, by which we are taught how to live; and the *anagogical*, by which we are taught how to cling to God. Therefore, the whole of sacred Scripture teaches these three truths: namely, the eternal generation and incarnation of Christ, the pattern of human life, and the union of the soul with God. The first is concerned with *faith;* the second with *morals;* and the third with the *ultimate goal of both.* The effort of the doctors should be aimed at the study of the first; that of the preachers, at the study of the second; that of the contemplatives, at the study of the third. The first is taught chiefly by Augustine; the second, by Gregory; the third, by Dionysius. Anselm follows Augustine; Bernard follows Gregory; Richard follows Dionysius. For Anselm excels in reasoning; Bernard, in preaching; Richard, in contemplation. But Hugh excels in all three.

6. From what has been said up to now it can be concluded that, according to our primary division, the light coming down from above is *fourfold;* nonetheless there are six differentiations of this light: namely, the light of *sacred Scripture*, the light of *sense perception*, the light of the *mechanical arts*, the light of *rational philosophy*, the light of *natural philosophy*, and the light of *moral philosophy*. Therefore, in the present life there are six illuminations; and they have their evening, for all *knowledge will be destroyed*. And therefore they will be followed by a seventh day of rest, a day which knows no evening, namely, *the illumination of glory.*

7. Therefore, these six illuminations may very fittingly be traced back to the six days of formation or illumination in which the world was made, so that the knowledge of sacred Scripture would correspond to the creation of the first day, that is, to the formation of light, and so on with the rest, one after the other in proper order. And as all those lights had their origin in a single light, so too all these branches of knowledge are ordered to the knowledge of sacred Scripture; they are contained in it; they are perfected by it; and they are ordered to the eternal illumination by means of it. Therefore all our knowledge should

quem illuminatio refertur in Deum, unde habuit ortum. Et ideo ibi completus est circulus, completus est senarius, et propterea status.

8. Videamus igitur, qualiter aliae illuminationes cognitionum reduci habent ad lumen sacrae Scripturae. Et primo videamus in illuminatione *cognitionis sensitivae*, quae tota versatur circa cognitionem sensibilium, ubi tria est considerare: cognoscendi *medium*, cognoscendi *exercitium*, cognoscendi *oblectamentum*. — Si consideremus *medium* cognoscendi, intuebimur ibi Verbum aeternaliter generatum et ex tempore incarnatum. Nullum enim sensibile movet potentiam cognitivam, nisi mediante similitudine, quae egreditur ab obiecto, sicut proles a parente; et hoc generaliter, realiter, vel exemplariter est necesse in omni sensu. Illa autem similitudo non tacit completionem in actu sentiendi, nisi uniatur cum organo et virtute; et cum unitur, nova fit perceptio, et per illam perceptionem fit reductio ad obiectum mediante similitudine illa. Et licet non semper obiectum sentiatur, semper tamen, quantum est de se, gignit similitudinem, cum est in sua completione. — Per hunc etiam modum intellige, quod a summa mente, quae cognoscibilis est interioribus sensibus mentis nostrae, aeternaliter emanavit similitudo, imago et proles; et ille postmodum, cum *venit plenitudo temporis*, unitus est menti et carni et hominis formam accepit, quod nunquam fuerat prius; et per illum omnes mentes nostrae reducuntur ad Deum, quae illam similitudinem Patris per fidem in corde suscipiunt.

9. Si vero consideremus sensum *exercitium*, intuebimur ibi *ordinem vivendi*. Unusquisque enim sensus se exercet circa proprium obiectum, refugit sibi nocivum et non usurpat alienum. — Per hunc modum tunc sensus *cordis* ordinate vivit, dum se ipsum exercet ad id, ad quod est, contra *negligentiam;* dum refugit sibi nocivum, contra *concupiscentiam:* et dum non usurpat sibi alienum, contra *superbiam.*

come to rest in the knowledge of sacred Scripture, and particularly in the *anagogical* understanding of Scripture through which any illumination is traced back to God from whom it took its origin. And there the circle is completed; the pattern of six is complete, and consequently there is rest.

8. Let us see, therefore, how the other illuminations of knowledge are to be traced back to the light of sacred Scripture. First, let us consider the illumination of *sense knowledge,* which is concerned exclusively with the knowledge of sensible objects. Here there are three elements to be considered: namely, the *medium* of knowledge, the *exercise* of knowledge, and the *delight* of knowledge. If we consider the *medium* of knowledge, we shall see there the Word begotten from all eternity and incarnate in time. Indeed, no sense object can stimulate the cognitive faculty except by means of a similitude which proceeds from the object as a child proceeds from its parent. And this procession by generation, whether in reality or in terms of exemplarity, is necessary for each of the senses. This similitude, however, does not complete the act of sense perception unless it is brought into contact with the sense organ and the sense faculty, and once that contact is established, there results a new perception. Through this perception the mind is led back to the object by means of that similitude. And even though the object is not always present to the senses, still it is the nature of the object that it always begets a similitude since this pertains to the fullness of its nature. In a similar way, understand that from the supreme Mind, which can be known by the inner senses of our mind, from all eternity there has emanated a Similitude, an Image, and an Offspring; and afterwards, when "the fulness of time came," He was united as never before to a mind and to flesh and assumed a human form. Through Him all our minds are led back to God when, through faith, we receive the Similitude of the Father into our hearts.

9. If we now consider the *exercise* of sense knowledge, we shall see in it *the pattern of human life,* for each sense acts in relation to its proper object, shrinks from what may harm it, and does not claim what is foreign to it. In the same way, the *inner sense* lives in an orderly way when it acts in reference to that which is proper to its nature, thus avoiding *negligence;* when it refrains from what is harmful, thus avoid-

Omnis enim inordinatio aut venit ex negligentia, aut ex concupiscentia, aut ex superbia. Ille enim ordinate vivit, qui vivit prudenter, temperanter et obtemperanter, ut refugiat negligentiam in operabilibus, concupiscentiam in appetibilibus, superbiam in excellentibus.

10. Si autem consideremus *oblectamentum,* intuebimur Dei et animae unionem. Omnis enim sensus suum sensibile conveniens quaerit cum desiderio, invenit cum gaudio, repetit sine fastidio, quia *non satiatur oculus visu, nec auris auditu impletur.* — Per hunc etiam modum sensus *cordis* nostri sive pulcrum, sive consonum, sive odoriferum, sive dulce, sive mulcebre debet desideranter quaerere, gaudenter invenire, incessanter repetere.— Ecce, quomodo in cognitione sensitiva continetur occulte divina sapientia, et quam mira est contemplatio quinque sensuum spiritualium secundum conformitatem ad sensus corporales.

11. Per hunc modum est reperire in illuminatione *artis mechanicae,* cuius tota intentio versatur circa *artificialium productionem.* In qua ista tria possumus intueri, scilicet *Verbi generationem* et *incarnationem, vivendi ordinem* et *Dei et animae foederationem.* Et hoc, si consideremus *egressum, effectum* et *fructum;* vel sic: *artem operandi, qualitatem effecti artificii* et *utilitatem fructus eliciti.*

12. Si consideremus *egressum,* videbimus, quod effectus artificialis exit ab artifice, mediante similitudine existente in mente; per quam artifex excogitat, antequam producat, et inde producit, sicut disposuit. Producit autem artifex exterius opus assimilatum exemplari interiori eatenus, qua potest melius; et si talem effectum posset producere, qui ipsum amaret et cognosceret, utique faceret; et si effectus ille cognosceret suum opificem, hoc esset mediante similitudine, secundum quam ab artifice processit; et si haberet obtenebratos oculos cognitionis, ut non posset supra se elevari, necesse esset ad hoc, ut ad

ing *concupiscence;* and when it refrains from claiming what does not belong to it, thus avoiding *pride.* For every disorder springs from neg-ligence, from concupiscence, or from pride. Surely then, a person who lives a prudent, temperate, and obedient life leads a well–ordered life; for in this way such a person avoids negligence with respect to things that ought to be done; concupiscence with respect to objects of desire; and pride with respect to matters of excellence.

⟂ interior light

10. Furthermore, if we consider the *delight* of sense knowledge, we shall see here the union of the soul with God. Indeed every sense seeks its proper sense object with longing, finds it with delight, and never wearied, seeks it again and again, because "the eye is not filled with seeing, neither is the ear filled with hearing." In the same way, our spiritual senses must seek with longing, find with joy, and time and again experience the beautiful, the harmonious, the fragrant, the sweet, or that which is delightful to the touch. Behold how the divine wisdom lies hidden in sense knowledge and how wonderful is the contemplation of the five spiritual senses in the light of their confor-mity to the bodily senses.

⟂ exterior light

11. In the same way divine wisdom may be found in the illu-mination of the *mechanical arts,* the sole purpose of which is the *produc-tion of artifacts.* In this illumination we can see the same three truths; namely, the *generation and incarnation of the Word,* the *pattern of human life,* and the *union of the soul with God.* And this is true if we consider the *production,* the *effect,* and the *fruit* of a work; or if we consider the *skill of the artist,* the *quality of the effect produced,* and the *usefulness of the prod-uct that results.*

12. If we consider the *production,* we shall see that the work of art proceeds from the artisan according to a similitude that exists in the mind. The artisan studies this pattern or model carefully before producing the artifact and then produces the object as planned. More-over the artisan produces an external work bearing the closest pos-sible resemblance to the interior exemplar. And if it were possible to produce an effect which could know and love the artisan, the artisan would certainly do this. And if that effect could know its maker, this would be by means of the similitude according to which it came from

cognitionem sui opificis duceretur, quod similitudo, per quam
productus esset effectus, condescenderet usque ad illam naturam, quae
ab eo posset capi et cognosci. — Per hunc modum intellige, quod a
summo Opifice nulla creatura processit nisi per Verbum aeternum," in
quo omnia disposuit", et per quod produxit non solum creaturas
habentes rationem *vestigii,* sed etiam *imaginis,* ut eidem assimilari
possint per cognitionem et amorem. Et quoniam per peccatum
rationalis creatura oculum contemplationis obnubilatum habuit;
decentissimum fuit, ut aeternum et invisibile fieret visibile et assumeret
carnem, ut nos ad Patrem reduceret. Et hoc est quod dicitur Ioannis
decimo quarto: *Nemo venit ad Patrem nisi per me;* et Matthaei undecimo:
Patrem nemo novit nisi Filius, et cui voluerit Filius revelare. Et ideo dicitur
Verbum caro factum. Considerantes igitur illuminationem artis
mechanicae quantum ad operis egressus, intuebimur ibi Verbum
generatum et incarnatum, id est Divinitatem et humanitatem et totius
fidei integritatem.

13. Si vero consideremus *effectum,* intuebimur *vivendi ordinem.*
Omnis enim artifex intendit producere opus pulcrum et utile et stabile; et tunc est carum et acceptabile opus, cum habet istas tres
conditiones. Iuxta haec tria necesse est reperiri tria in ordine vivendi,
scilicet *"scire, velle* et impermutabiliter sive *perseveranter operari." Scientia*
reddit opus pulcrum, *voluntas* reddit utile, *perseverantia* reddit stabile.
Primum est in rationali, secundum in concupiscibili, tertium in irascibili.

14. Si consideremus fructum, inveniemus *Dei et animae unionem.*
Omnis enim artifex, qui aliquod opus facit, aut facit, ut per illud
laudetur, aut ut per illud sibi aliquid *operetur* vel lucretur, aut ut in illo
delectetur, secundum tria, quae sunt in appetibilibus, scilicet bonum
honestum, conferens et *delectabile.* Propter haec tria fecit Deus animam
rationalem, ut ipsa eum *laudaret,* ut ipsa illi *serviret,* ut ipsa in eo

the hands of the artisan. And if the eyes of its understanding were so darkened that it could not be elevated above itself in order to come to a knowledge of its maker, it would be necessary for the similitude according to which the effect was produced to lower itself to that sort of nature which the effect could grasp and know. In like manner, understand that no creature has proceeded from the most high Creator except through the eternal Word, " in whom God has disposed all things," and by which Word God has produced creatures bearing not only the nature of a *vestige* but also that of an *image* so that through knowledge and love creatures might become like God. And since by sin the rational creature had dimmed the eye of contemplation, it was most fitting that the eternal and invisible should become visible and assume flesh in order to lead us back to God. Indeed, this is what is related in the fourteenth chapter of Saint John: "No one comes to the Father but through me," and in the eleventh chapter of Saint Matthew: "No one knows the Son except the Father; nor does anyone know the Father except the Son, and those to whom the Son chooses to reveal him." For that reason, then, it is said, "the Word was made flesh." Therefore, considering the illumination of the mechanical arts as regards the production of the work, we shall see there the Word begotten and incarnate, that is, the divinity and the humanity and the integrity of all faith.

13. If we consider the *effect*, we shall see there the *pattern of human life.* Every artisan aims to produce a work that is beautiful, useful, and enduring; and only when it possesses these three qualities is the work highly valued and acceptable. It is necessary to find three parallel elements in the pattern of life: *"to know, to will,* and *to work constantly with perseverance." Knowledge* makes a work beautiful; the *will* makes it useful; and *perseverance* makes it lasting. The first resides in the rational, the second in the concupiscible, and the third in the irascible appetite.

14. If we consider the *fruit,* we shall find there *the union of the soul with God,* for every artisan who fashions a work does so in order to derive *praise, benefit,* or *delight* from it — a threefold purpose which corresponds to the three formal objects of the appetites: namely, a *noble* good, a *useful* good, and an *agreeable* good. It was for these three reasons that God made the soul rational, namely, that of its own accord, it

delectaretur et quiesceret; et hoc est per caritatem, *in qua qui manet in Deo manet, et Deus in eo,* ita quod est ibi quaedam mirabilis unio et ex unione mirabilis delectatio; quoniam, secundum quod dicitur in Proverbiis, *deliciae meae esse cum filiis hominum.* Ecce, quomodo illuminatio artis mechanicae via est ad illuminationem sacrae Scripturae, et nihil est in ea, quod non praedicet veram sapientiam, et ideo sacra Scriptura frequenter talibus similitudinibus utitur satis recte.

15. Iuxta hunc etiam modum est reperire in illuminatione *rationalis philosophiae,* cuius principalis intentio versatur circa *sermonem.* In quo est tria considerare secundum triplicem ipsius sermonis considerationem, scilicet respectu *proferentis,* ratione *prolationis* et respectu *audientis* sive ratione finis.

16. Si sermonem consideremus in respectu ad *loquentem,* sic videmus, quod omnis sermo significat *mentis conceptum,* et ille conceptus interior est verbum mentis et eius proles, quae nota est etiam ipsi concipienti. Sed ad hoc, quod fiat nota audienti induit formam vocis, et verbum intelligibile mediante illo indumento fit sensibile et auditur exterius et suscipitur in aure cordis audientis, et tamen non recedit a mente proferentis. — Iuxta hunc modum videmus in Verbo aeterno, quod Pater aeternaliter ipsum concepit generando, secundum illud Proverbiorum octavo: *Nondum erant abyssi, et ego iam concepta eram.* Sed ad hoc, quod homini sensuali fieret cognoscibile, induit formam carnis, *et Verbum caro factum est et habitavit in nobis,* et tamen remansit *in sinu Patris.*

17. Si vero consideremus sermonem ratione *sui,* sic intuebimur in eo ordinem vivendi. Ad complementum enim sermonis necessario ista tria concurrunt, scilicet *congruitas, veritas,* et *ornatus.* — Et iuxta haec tria omnis actio nostra debet habere *modum, speciem* et *ordinem;* ut sit *modificata* per modestiam in exteriori opere, *speciosa* per munditiam in affectione, *ordinata* et ornata per rectitudinem in intentione. Tunc enim recte et ordinate vivitur, cum est intentio recta, affectio munda et

might *praise* God, *serve* God, find *delight* in God, and be at rest; and this takes place through charity. "Those who abide in charity, abide in God, and God in them," in such a way that there is found a kind of wondrous union and from that union comes a wondrous delight, for in the Book of Proverbs it is written, "My delight was to be with the children of men." Behold how the illumination of the mechanical arts is a path to the illumination of sacred Scripture. There is nothing there which does not manifest true wisdom, and for this reason sacred Scripture quite rightly makes frequent use of such similitudes.

15. In a similar way divine wisdom is to be found in the illumination of *rational philosophy* whose principal concern is *speech*. Here three elements are to be considered which correspond to three aspects of speech itself: namely, the *person speaking*, the *delivery* of the speech, and the *hearer* or the goal.

16. Considering speech in relation to the *speaker*, we see that all speech signifies a *mental concept*. That inner concept is the word of the mind and its offspring which is known to the person conceiving it. But in order that this concept may become known to the hearer, it assumes the form of the voice; and by means of this clothing, the intelligibile word becomes sensible and is heard externally. It is received into the ear of listener and yet does not depart from the mind of the person uttering it. It is something like this that we see in the Eternal Word. God conceived the Word by an eternal act of generation, as it is written in the eighth chapter of the Book of Proverbs, "The depths were not as yet, and I was already conceived." But that the Word might be known by human beings who are endowed with senses, the Word assumed the form of flesh, and "the Word was made flesh and dwelt among us," while remaining "in the bosom of God."

17. Considering speech in the light of its *delivery*, we shall see there the pattern of *human life*, for three essential qualities work together for the perfection of speech: namely, *fittingness*, *truth*, and *style*. Corresponding to these three qualities, all acts of ours should be characterized by *measure*, *beauty*, and *order* so that they may be *measured* by reason of modesty in external works, *rendered beautiful* by purity of affection, and *ordered* and adorned by uprightness of intention. For

operatio modesta.

18. Si vero consideremus sermonem ratione finis, sic est ad *exprimendum*, ad *erudiendum* et ad *movendum*, sed nunquam *exprimit* aliquid, nisi mediante specie, nunquam *docet*, nisi mediante lumine arguente, nunquam *movet*, nisi mediante virtute; et constat, quod hoc non fit nisi per speciem et lumen et virtutem intrinsecam, intrinsecus *animae unita*: et ideo concludit Augustinus, quod ille solus est verus doctor, qui potest speciem imprimere et lumen infundere et virtutem dare cordi audientis. Et hinc est, quod "cathedram habet in caelo qui intus corda docet."— Sicut ergo nihil cognoscitur per sermonem perfecte, nisi mediante virtute, lumine et specie unitis animae, sic ad hoc, quod anima erudiatur ad Dei cognitionem per ipsius internam locutionem, necesse est, quod uniatur ei *qui est splendor gloriae et figura substantiae eius, portans omnia verbo virtutis suae.* — Ex quo patet, quam mira est haec contemplatio, per quam Augustinus in multis libris manuducit ad divinam sapientiam.

19. Secundum etiam hunc modum est reperire in illuminatione *naturali philosophiae,* cuius principalis intentio versatur circa *rationes formales* in *materia, in anima* et in *divina sapientia.* Quas tripliciter contingit considerare, scilicet secundum *habitudinem proportionis,* secundum *effectum causalitalis* et secundum *medium unionis,* et secundum haec tria est reperire tria praemissa.

20. Si consideremus eas secundum *habitudinem proportionis,* videbimus in eis *Verbum aeternum* et *Verbum incarnatum.* Rationes *intellectuales* et abstractae quasi mediae sunt inter *seminales* et *ideales.* Sed rationes *seminales* non possunt esse in *materia,* quin sit in ea generatio et productio formae; similiter nec in *anima* rationes *intellectuales,* quin sit generatio verbi in mente; ergo nec *ideales in Deo,* quin sit productio Verbi a Patre secundum rectam proportionem; hoc enim est dignitatis, et si convenit creaturae, multo fortius inferri potest

then truly does one live an upright and well–ordered life when one's intention is upright, one's affection pure, and one's activity within its proper limit.

18. If we consider speech in relation to its *purpose*, we find that it aims to *express*, to *instruct*, and to *persuade*. But it never *expresses* except by means of a likeness; it never *teaches* except by means of a convincing light; it never *persuades* except by power; and it is evident that these effects are accomplished only by means of an inherent likeness, light, and power intrinsically *united to the soul*. Therefore, Augustine concludes that the only true teacher is one who can impress a likeness, infuse light, and grant power to the heart of the hearer. Hence it is that "the one who teaches within hearts has a chair in heaven." Now as nothing can be known perfectly by means of speech except by reason of a power, a light, and a likeness united to the soul, so, too, for the soul to be instructed in the knowledge of God by interior conversation with the divine there is required a union with the one who is "the brightness of the divine glory and the image of the divine substance, upholding all things by the word of divine power." From this it becomes clear how wonderful is this contemplation by which Augustine in his many writings leads us by the hand to divine wisdom.

19. By the same line of reasoning the wisdom of God is to be found in the illumination of *natural philosophy*, which is concerned chiefly with the *formal principles* in *matter*, in the *soul*, and in the *divine wisdom*. These should be considered from three perspectives: namely, as regards the *relation of proportion*, the *effect of causality*, and the *medium of union*. And in these three can be found the three concerns mentioned above.

20. If we consider the formal principles in terms of their *relation of proportion*, we shall see there the *Word Eternal* and the *Word Incarnate*. The *intellectual* and abstract principles are, as it were, midway between the *seminal* and the *ideal* principles. But *seminal* principles cannot exist in *matter* without generation and the production of form; neither can *intellectual* principles exist in the *soul* without the generation of a word in the mind. Therefore, *ideal* principles cannot exist *in God* without the generation of the Word from the Father in due proportion.

de Creatore. Propter quod dixit Augustinus, quod Filius Dei est "ars Patris ". — Rursus, appetitus, qui est in materia, ordinatur ad rationes intellectuales, ut nullo modo perfecta sit generatio, nisi anima rationalis uniatur materiae corporali. — Per similem igitur rationem potest argui, quod summa perfectio et nobilissima in universo esse non possit, nisi natura, in qua sunt rationes seminales, et natura, in qua sunt rationes intellectuales, et natura, in qua sunt rationes ideales, simul concurrant in unitatem personae, quod factum est in Filii Dei incarnatione. Praedicat igitur tota naturalis philosophia per habitudinem proportionis Dei Verbum natum et incarnatum, ut idem sit *alpha et omega*, natum scilicet in principio et ante tempora, incarnatum vero in fine saeculorum.

21. Si vero consideremus rationes istas secundum *effectum causalitatis*, perpendemus *ordinem vivendi*: quoniam generatio non potest fieri in materia generabili et corruptibili secundum rationes seminales nisi beneficio luminis corporum supercaelestium, quae elongantur a generatione et corruptione, scilicet a *sole, luna* et *stellis*. — Per hunc etiam modum anima non potest opera viva facere, nisi suscipiat a sole, id est a Christo, gratuiti luminis beneficium, et nisi consequatur ipsius lunae, id est Virginis Mariae, Matris Christi patrocinium, et nisi imitetur aliorum Sanctorum exempla; ex quorum concursu congregetur in ipsa opus vivum atque perfectum. Unde ordo vivendi pendet in tribus.

22. Si autem consideremus istas rationes secundum *unionis medium*, intelligemus, per quem modum fiat *unio animae ad Deum*. Nam natura corporalis animae non potest uniri, nisi mediante humore, mediante spiritu et mediante calore, quae tria disponunt carnem, ut vitam suscipiat ab anima. — Secundum hoc etiam intelligitur, quod Deus non praestat vitam animae et unitur, nisi sit *humida* per gemitum compunctionis et pietatis, nisi sit *spiritualis* per contemptum omnis terrenitatis, nisi sit *calida* per desiderium patriae caelestis et ipsius dilecti. — Ecce, qualiter in philosophia naturali latet sapientia Dei.

Truly, this is a mark of dignity; and if it is true of the creature, how much more so must it be true of the Creator. This is the reason why Augustine said that the Son of God is the "art of the Father." Again, the natural tendency in matter is so ordered to the intellectual principles that generation would not be perfect without the union of the rational soul with the material body. By similar reasoning, therefore, we come to the conclusion that the highest and noblest perfection cannot exist in this world unless that nature in which the seminal principles are present, and that nature in which the intellectual principles are present, and that nature in which the ideal principles are present are simultaneously brought together in the unity of one person, as was done in the incarnation of the Son of God. Therefore all natural philosophy, by reason of the relation of proportion, presupposes the Word of God as begotten and incarnate, the *Alpha* and the *Omega*, that is, begotten in the beginning before all time, and incarnate in the fulness of time.

21. Now if we consider these causes according to the *effect of causality*, we shall be considering the *pattern of human life*, since generation by means of seminal principles cannot take place in generative and corruptible matter except by the beneficial action of the light of those heavenly bodies that are most remote from generation and corruption; namely, the *sun*, the *moon*, and the *stars*. So too the soul can perform no living works unless it receive from the sun, that is, from Christ, the gift of a gratuitous light; unless it seek the protection of the moon, that is, of the Virgin Mary, Mother of Christ; and unless it imitate the example of the other saints. When all these concur, a living and perfect work is accomplished in the soul. Therefore the right order of living depends on these three influences.

22. Moreover, if we consider these causes with respect to the *medium of union*, we shall understand how the *union of the soul with God* takes place, for the corporal nature can be united to the soul only through the medium of moisture, breath, and warmth: three conditions which dispose the flesh to receive life from the soul. So too we may understand that God gives life to the soul and is united to it only on the condition that it be *moistened* with tears of compunction and filial love, that it be made *spiritual* by contempt of every earthly thing,

23. Penes modos praedictos est reperire in illuminatione *philosophiae moralis* lumen *sacrae Scripturae:* quoniam intentio moralis philosophiae principaliter versatur circa rectitudinem; versatur enim circa iustitiam generalem, quae, ut dicit Anselmus, "est rectitudo voluntatis." Rectum autem habet tripliciter notificari, et secundum hoc tria praemissa lucent in consideratione rectitudinis. Uno modo dicitur "*rectum*, cuius medium non exit ab extremis." Si ergo in Deo est summa rectitudo et secundum se, et in quantum est principium, et in quantum est finis omnium; necesse est in Deo ponere mediam personam *secundum se*, ut una sit tantum producens, alia tantum producta, media vero producens et producta. Necesse est etiam ponere medium *in egressu et regressu* rerum; sed medium *in egressu* necesse est, quod plus teneat se a parte producentis, medium vero *in regressu*, plus a parte redeuntis; sicut ergo res exierunt a Deo per Verbum Dei, sic ad completum reditum necesse est, Mediatorem *Dei et hominum* non tantum Deum esse, sed etiam hominem, ut homines reducat ad Deum.

24. Alio modo dicitur *rectum* quod dirigenti se conformatur. Et secundum hoc in consideratione rectitudinis conspicitur *ordo vivendi.* Ille enim recte vivit, qui dirigitur secundum regulas iuris divini. Et hoc est, quando voluntas hominis assentit *praeceptis* necessariis, *monitis* salutiferis, *consiliis* perfectis, ut probet homo, *quae sit voluntas Dei bona et beneplacens et perfecta.* Et tunc est rectus ordo vivendi, in quo nulla obliquitas potest reperiri.

25. Tertio modo dicitur *rectum* cuius summitas est sursum erecta, sicut homo habet staturam rectam. Et secundum hoc in consideratione rectitudinis manifestatur *Dei et animae unio.* Cum enim Deus sit sursum, necesse est, quod apex ipsius mentis sursum erigatur. Hoc autem est, cum *rationalis* assentit primae veritati propter se et su-

and that it *be warmed* by desire for its heavenly home and its Beloved. Behold how the wisdom of God lies hidden in natural philosophy.

23. In the same way the light of *sacred Scripture* is to be found in the illumination of *moral philosophy*. Since moral philosophy is concerned principally with rectitude, it treats of general justice which Saint Anselm calls the "rectitude of the will." The term *right* has three meanings, and accordingly the three central ideas already mentioned come to light in the consideration of rectitude. In one sense of the word, something is said to be *"right (=straight)* if its middle is not out of line with its extreme points." If then God is perfect rectitude by virtue of the divine nature itself, and since God is the Beginning and the End of all things, it is necessary to posit within God an intermediate person of the *divine nature*, so that there may be one person who only produces, another who is only produced, but an intermediary who both produces and is produced. It is also necessary to posit an intermediary in the *going forth* and in the *return* of things: in the *going forth*, a medium which will be closer to the productive principle; in the *return*, a medium which will be closer to the one returning. Therefore, as creatures went forth from God by the Word of God, so for a perfect return, it was necessary that the Mediator *between God and humanity* be not only God but also human so that this mediator might lead humanity back to God.

24. In another sense, that is called *right* which is conformed to that by which it is ruled. Accordingly, when rectitude is viewed from this perspective, the *rule of life* is discerned. For that person indeed lives rightly who is guided by the regulations of the divine law. This is the case when the will of a human person accepts necessary *precepts*, salutary *warnings*, and *counsels* of perfection and thus demonstrates what is *the good and acceptable and perfect will of God*. And then the order of life is right when nothing can be found to be out of line.

25. In the third sense, something is called *right* when its summit is raised upward, as in the case of a human being with its upright posture. And in this sense, in the consideration of rectitude there is manifested the *union of the soul with God*, for since God is above, it

pra omnia, cum *irascibilis* innititur summae largitati, et cum *concupiscibilis* adhaeret bonitati; tunc qui hoc modo *Deo adhaeret unus spiritus est.*

26. Et sic patet, quomodo *multiformis sapientia Dei,* quae lucide traditur in sacra Scriptura, occultatur in omni cognitione et in omni natura. Patet etiam, quomodo omnes cognitiones famulantur theologiae; et ideo ipsa assumit exempla et utitur vocabulis pertinentibus ad omne genus cognitionis. Patet etiam, quam ampla sit via illuminativa, et quomodo in omni re, quae sentitur sive quae cognoscitur, interius lateat ipse Deus. — Et hic est fructus omnium scientiarum, ut in omnibus aedificetur fides, *honorificetur Deus,* componantur mores, hauriantur consolationes, quae sunt in unione sponsi et sponsae, quae quidem fit per caritatem, ad quam terminatur tota intentio sacrae Scripturae, et per consequens omnis illuminatio desursum descendens, et sine qua omnis cognitio vana est, quia nunquam pervenitur ad Filium nisi per Spiritum sanctum, qui docet nos *omnem veritatem; qui est benedictus in saecula saeculorum. Amen.*

necessarily follows that the apex of the mind itself must be raised aloft. And indeed this is what actually happens when our *rational nature* assents to the first truth for its own sake and above all things, when our *irascible nature* strives after the highest generosity, and when our *concupiscible nature* clings to the good. One who keeps close to God in this way *is one spirit with God.*

26. And so it is evident how the *manifold wisdom of God,* which is clearly revealed in sacred Scripture, lies hidden in all knowledge and in all nature. It is clear also how all divisions of knowledge are servants of theology, and it is for this reason that theology makes use of illustrations and terms pertaining to every branch of knowledge. It is likewise clear how wide the illuminative way may be, and how the divine reality itself lies hidden within everything which is perceived or known . And this is the fruit of all sciences, that in all, faith may be strengthened, *God may be honored,* character may be formed, and consolation may be derived from union of the Spouse with the beloved, a union which takes place through charity: a charity in which the whole purpose of sacred Scripture, and thus of every illumination descending from above, comes to rest — a charity without which all knowledge is vain because no one comes to the Son except through the Holy Spirit who teaches us *all the truth, who is blessed forever. Amen.*